Human Skeletal Assemblage from the Harappan Site of Farmana

A Bio-archaeological Analysis

Human Skeletal Assemblage from the Harappan Site of Farmana

A Bio-archaeological Analysis

Veena Mushrif-Tripathy
Vasant Shinde

Kaveri Books
New Delhi - 110 002

First Published in 2019
ISBN : 978-81-7479-223-5

Published by
Kaveri Books
4832/24, Ansari Road, Daryaganj,
New Delhi - 110 002 (India)
Ph. : 011- 4707 2321
E-mail : info@kaveribooks.com
kaveribooks@gmail.com
Website : www.kaveribooks.com

Typesetting at Creative Graphics, Delhi

PRINTED IN INDIA

Foreword

The accidental discovery of the Harappan culture in Indian sub-continent almost a century ago dramatically changed the perspectives in Indian ancient history. This culture covers a wide geographical area extending from Baluchistan on the west to beyond Delhi into the interfluves on the east and from the eastern foot of the Suleiman mountain range in the north to the Tapti estuary in the south. Sites like Harappa, Mohenjodaro, Kalibangan, Dholavira, Lothal, etc. gives extensive evidence of their spread and civilization. Newly discovered sites like Sanuali, Rakhigarhi and Farmana (and even the smaller sites like Padri) have demonstrated the potential to understand this culture in further detail. Deccan College Post-Graduate and Research Institute, Pune have contributed substantially for deciphering the life ways of these populations.

The site of Farmana was excavated by Deccan College Post Graduate and Research Institute, Pune and Maharshi Dayanand University, Rohtak, (under the aegis of the Archaeological Survey of India). The excavations carried out at the site have revealed two distinct phases of the Harappan Culture: Early Harappan and the Mature Harappan. The site of Farmana is one of the few Harappan sites in the subcontinent that has Mature Harappan cemetery located in its vicinity. Remains of seventy burials were uncovered. Also, there are a few burials, the pit-lines of which have been traced and numbered, but not excavated. The pottery and other antiquities found in burials clearly indicate that these burials are comparable with cemetery R-37 found at Harappa. Anthropological findings on the skeletal remains of 35 individuals are reported in this monograph.

Prof. Vasant Shinde and Dr. Veena Mushrif-Tripathy are experts in their own areas of research. Prof. Shinde is one of the most respected scholars in the field of Indian protohistory. He was personally involved in the excavation of the site of Farmana. His experience and awareness of the research potential of osseous remains prompted him to give meticulous attention to the recovery of human skeletons from the site, which proved useful to read the anthropological data in proper cultural perspective. Dr. Veena Mushrif-Tripathy has studied several archaeological human skeletal series representing various cultural levels and covering a very wide geographical region. She has earned reputation in the subject over these years. I am happy to see that these two scholars are coming together for completing a thorough study of the human skeletons from Farmana. Dr. Veena Mushrif-Tripathy has given provided a very comprehensive account of the demographic and pathological profile of the Harappan Farmana population. I am sure this analysis will earn the applause of the academic world.

I am honoured by the request of Prof. Shinde and Dr. Veena Mushrif-Tripathy to write foreword to this book.

Prof. Subhash Walimbe

Acknowledgments

Authors like to thank everyone who helped in the preparation of this monograph. The excavation of Framana started in 2008-09. The human skeletal material was stored in the Anthropology Laboratory, Deccan College Post Graduate, and Research Institute, Pune 411 006. With the funding from University Grant commission, this project was completed during 2011 to 2013. We are thankful to University Grant Commission for funding this work. We also like to thank Dr. Manmohan Kumar (retired faculty), Dayanand University, Rohtak, Haryana for collaborating with Deccan College for the excavation and providing local support.

We appreciate Dr. Vivek Dangi for his helping hand during the excavation of the cemetery at Farmana. During the period of analysis, it became easier as Mr. K. Chakravorthy, who was Project fellow in this major research project helped in generating the database.

We like to thank Professor Toshiki Osada and Dr. Akinori Usugi from Research Institute for Humanity and Nature Kyoto, Japan and other delegates from their institute who participated in the Farmana excavation. Authors also thank Dr. Benjamin Valentine and Dr. John Krigman for conducting the dental isotopic analysis.

We would also like to thank all the participants in the exaction and researcher who helped in the collection of skeleton data from the cemetery. We would like to mention few of them including Dr. Amol Kulkarni, Mr. Nilesh Jadhav, Dr. Amruta Sarkar-Das, Dr. Kim and Mr. Dighe. We also thank Mr. Devadatta Phule for the line drawing of skull 39b which is used on the front page of this monograph.

Veena Mushrif-Tripathy
Vasant Shinde

Contents

List of Tables

List of Figures

1

Farmana and Its Cultural Sequence

The present chapter deals with the general introduction of the site Farmana and the description of the cemetery. The information is taken from earlier published reports (Shinde *et al* 2009, 2011).

The ancient site of Farmana (29°02'22"N and 76°18'21"E) falls in the jurisdiction of three different villages—Farmana, Seman and Bhaini Chandrapal (Badi Bahen) all in the jurisdiction of Meham block of Rohtak district in the state of Haryana, which is locally known as Daksh Kheda (Fig. 1.1). Since a major portion of this site lies in the jurisdiction of Farmana village, it is considered as a part of that village. The site is 4 km to the west of Farmana on the metal road between Farmana and Seman with the Chautang river basin. There are lakes in this vicinity of the site. The Harappans may have relied on such lakes for their water necessity. A survey revealed that a very extensive area measuring over 18 hectares in size was under occupation (Shinde et al. 2008 a-b). The major portions of the site particularly along the periphery and also the upper levels of the Mature Harappan period have been destroyed as the entire site is under cultivation. The total habitation deposit survived now, varies from 2.5 m to 3.5 m.

The site was excavated by Deccan College Post Graduate and Research Institute, Pune in collaboration with the Research Institute for Humanities and Nature, Kyoto, Japan and Maharshi Dayanand University, Rohtak, under the aegis of the Archaeological Survey of India. Excavations carried out in the first season (2006-07) revealed pit dwelling in the Early Harappan levels and a gradual transformation to rectangular mud-brick structures and complexes in ascending order. Second season's (2007-08) excavation was mainly confined to the uppermost level in the central part of the site. Many structural remains consist of the main street, two small streets and three multi-roomed complexes were uncovered. The most noteworthy find of the season (2007-08) includes one steatite seal bearing a Zebu bull with prominent dewlap with the large terracotta amulet stamped with a unicorn and Harappan letters. A Harappan cemetery was found at a distance of 900 m to the northwest of the site.

The excavations carried out at the site has revealed two distinct phases of the Harappan Culture: Early Harappan (Period-1- Regional Hakra Culture) and the Mature Harappan (represented by three sub-phases-Period-IIA, IIB, and IIC). The site which was in the form of a prominent mound some 50 years ago is being constantly used by the farmers for cultivation. It has resulted in the damage of entire Early Historic, Painted Grey Ware, Late Harappan and part of the upper Mature Harappan (Period-11C) levels. The damage is so extensive that the structural remains and features are found immediately below the ploughing zone.

Cultural Sequence

The site is located on an elevated natural silt deposit, which is layer (13). Above this is a habitational deposit, which has survived between 2.5 to 3.5 m. In all, twelve habitation layers have been observed within Farmana deposit. Two periods of the Harappan cultures have survived at the site. They are as follows:

Period- I : It is Early Harappan (Regional Hakra Culture Tradition) dated to 3500-2600 BCE. Most of the dates for this period are quite early as at Bhirrana and therefore safe to presume that the Early Harappans flourished in this part in the middle of 4th millennium BC and continued until the emergence of the Mature Harappan phase around 2600 BCE.

The kind of pottery, structures and other material recovered from the site of Farmana is reported from other sites like Bhirrana (Rao, *et al.* 2004-05), Girawad (Shinde, *et al.* 2008a) and Kunal (Khatri and Acharya 1995). The excavated evidence from these sites suggests that the early settlers began their lifestyle with modest dwellings consisting of mostly underground structures, either circular or oval in shape dug in natural soil. Post-holes were noticed on the periphery suggesting there were superstructures on these pit-dwellings. The evidence of charred bones, cooking pottery along with fine variety in them is indicative of their use for dwelling purposes.

They used very advanced pottery making and firing technology and produced a variety of wares such as Mud Appliqué, Incised, Chocolate Slipped, Reserve Slipped, Grooved, etc. The copper and lapidary crafts were well developed indicating people had already developed long-distance trade contacts for acquiring suitable raw materials and circulating finished goods. This, no doubt, suggests that the first settlers came to the site from elsewhere with ready craft technology.

The excavation carried out at Farmana and a few other sites in the Ghaggar basin revealed that the early culture remained rural in character. The urbanization was a gradual process in this region and it was fully achieved only in the Mature Harappan phase in the middle of the third millennium BCE. As limited excavation was carried out in the Early levels at the site, it is difficult to comment on their lifestyle including social and economic aspects in details.

Period- II : Mature Harappan (sub-divided into Period-IIA, Period- IIB and Period-IIC)

The Mature Harappan period at the site is represented by a thick deposit of more than two meters. A large number of artifacts, pottery, and structures of this period have been excavated. There appears to be some variation in the material remains from the beginning to the end of the Mature Harappan occupation at the site. This variation coupled with stratigraphy, enable identification of sub-phases. This sub-phase is quite clear in their burials. The Mature Harappan therefore has been sub-divided into Period-1A, Period-IIB, and Period-IIC. No radiocarbon or AMS dates are yet available for this period, but tentatively on the basis of the study of data from the site as well as on comparative analysis Period-IIA can be dated between 2600-2400 BCE, Period-IIB from 2400-2200 BCE and Period- IIC, which has been completely scooped out from the site can be dated between 2200-2000 BCE. This division of the Mature Harappan period and dating will have to be supported by additional data and dates. Tentatively layers 6-9 could be assigned to Period-IIA and 1-5 to Period-IIB. No layers of the last Mature Harappan period have survived at the site.

The Mature Harappan period at the site marks the culmination of the cultural process that began in the early stage, which is reflected in their settlement pattern and cultural material. The entire 18 ha area was occupied during this period suggesting an expansion of the population and attainment of prosperity. There is a gradual transition from Early Harappan to the Mature Harappan at the site which is clearly evident in their structures and pottery. The pit-dwelling in the lowermost level was replaced by mud-brick rectangular structures in the subsequent levels. Between the pit-dwellings and the beginning of the Mature Harappan phase (IIA), a number of floor levels are noticed indicating gradual development. In the level between Early Harappan and Mature Harappan, which can also be termed as Transition, are found small rectangular possibly independent structures with circular fireplaces. Elaborate remains of well-planned mud bricks and burnt-brick structural complexes, streets, drainages, rectangular fireplaces and storage areas came into existence.

The brick size that was used right from the Early Harappan until the end of Period IIB is in the ratio of 1:2:4. The so-called Early Harappan brick ratio of 1:2:3 is almost absent in the Ghaggar basin, except at the site of Banawali in Hissar District (Bisht 1993), which was excavated on a large scale. Large horizontal area of Period IIB has unearthed a part of the well-planned settlement of the Mature Harappan people at Farmana. Partially handmade and un-refined pottery found in the Early Harappan period was refining gradually and became superior ceramic assemblage with more typical Harappan shapes in the Mature Harappan phase. The classical painted Harappan Red ware makes its appearance. The seals are completely absent in Period-I but appear from the beginning of Period-II. The presence of seal and sealing, elaborate evidence for town planning, rich cultural material excavated so far, advanced technology and practice of elaborate burial customs during Period- II all point towards the attainment of urbanization in this period.

The Cemetery at the Site

There are many sites in the Ghaggar basin such as Kalibangan, Rakhigarhi, Tarkhanewala Dera, Sanauli, Bedwa, Putti Semen, etc. where Harappan cemeteries were discovered. It is now confirmed that the cemetery at Bedwa, Putti Seman, and Sanauli belong to the Late Harappan period, whereas Kalibangan, Rakhigarhi, and Tarkhanewala Dera have Mature Harappan cemeteries same as that found at Farmana. The site of Farmana is one of the few Harappan sites in Indian Subcontinent having its cemetery in the proximity (Fig. 1.2). The Harappan cemetery at Farmana was discovered accidentally when the owner of the land (Mr. Ramdhari from Seman village) was ploughing this land for lifting the soil. Two burials were destroyed in the process of digging. The prompt action from Department of History, M.D. University, Rohtak, brought this discovery to the notice. In 2007-08 season seven burials were excavated (Shinde *et al.* 2008b, 2010, 2011). The preliminary survey had indicated its spread over a large area (approximately 3 ha). The cemetery is located to the northwest of the habitation site at a distance of 900 m from the datum point located in the center of the habitation site. It is located on the right hand (north) of the Farmana-Seman motorable road.

Figure 1.1: Location of Farmana with other Harappan sites

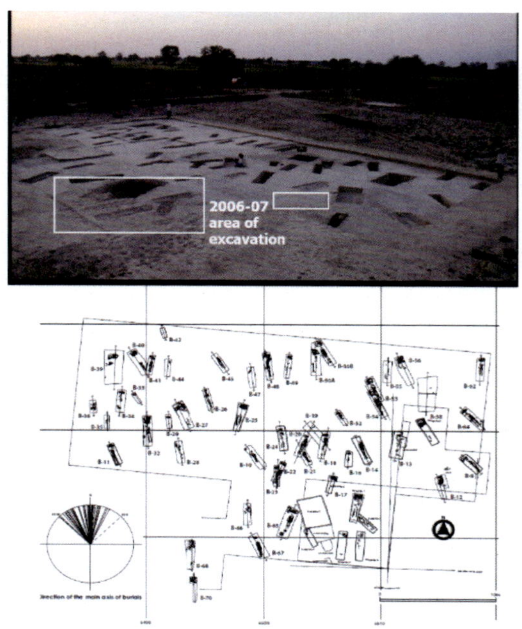

Figure 1.2: General view of Farmana Cemetery

Two trenches measuring 7 m by 7 m were laid in the selected portion. On scraping in these trenches, the outlines of burial pits became clear. The burial pits were dug in the natural alluvial soil, which is brownish/ yellowish in colour. The colour of the soil, filled after placing dead bodies in them, turned slightly greyish/ blackish in colour, which was very easy to distinguish from the natural soil. Remains of seven burials were uncovered in these two trenches, six located in the western trench (Trench 1) and one in the eastern trench (Trench 2) (Figures 1.3 and 1.4). On the basis of burial goods and the nature of pits, Burials nos. 1, 6 and 7 appear to be either of rich persons or of those whose status in the society was high (Shinde *et al* 2009).

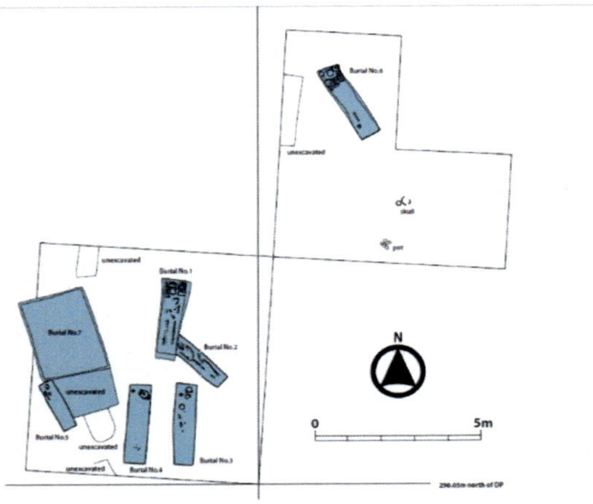

Figure 1.3: Line drawing of excavation in 2007-08

Figure 1.4: Cemetery excavation in 2007-08

In order to understand various customs and socio-religious aspects of the Harappans from the burials, it was decided to excavate cemetery at Farmana on the much larger scale in 2008-09. The aim was to know about the population staying at the site from an anthropological perspective. This analysis included extraction of the ancient DNA, isotope investigation and understanding the health and diet of inhabitants. All together remains of seventy burials were uncovered in the area spread over 35 m X 21 m. Also, there were few burials, of which the pit-lines have been traced and numbered, but did not excavate. The burial pits have three different orientations- northwest-southeast, north-south, and northeast-southwest. On the basis of the pottery and ornaments found along these burials, their chronological positions have become clear. They belong to three different sub-phases of the Mature Harappan period.

A number of trenches were laid out in an effort to expose a large part of the Harappan Cemetery at Farmana. These trenches were located to the east, west, north, and south of the burials (1-7) initially excavated in the 2007-08 season. The trenches in the cemetery measured 7 × 7 m. They were given labels that combine numerals with alphabetic symbols. The alphabetical signs increase from east to west from the datum point. Numerical signs increase towards the north from the datum point. This method is similar to that used in the habitation area, except in the cemetery "C" was added as a prefix to the alphabetic symbols to differentiate cemetery from habitation. The datum point at the burial site is located 37.5 m to the east and 3.5 m to the south of the northern end of the ditch dug by the owner of the field for lifting soil. The numbering of the trenches accommodates all sides of the datum point though a majority of the trenches lie between the east-west and north-south line of the datum. One trench line each extends to the south and east of the datum line. Trench CA1 lies to the southeast corner of the datum line whereas CB1, CC1, CD1, CE1, CF1, CG1 and CH1lie to the south of the east-west datum line.

Trenches CA2, CA3 and CA4 lie to the east of the north-south datum line. Trenches CB2, CC2, CE2, CF2, CG2 and CH2 are located to the west of the datum line. The next two lines of trenches, namely CB3, CC3, CD3, CE3, CF3, CG3, CH3, and CB4, CC4, CD4, and CE4, CF4, CG4, CH4, are to the north of the trenches located to the west of the datum point of the trenches mentioned above. CF2, CD3, CE3, CF3, CG3, CH3, CD4, CE4, CF4, CG4, CH4 were selected for excavation. A small portion of trench CG1 and CG2 was also excavated as the burial no 69 lies on the junction between them. To determine how far the cemetery extends to the north, one trench 35 m to the north of CD4 to CH4 lines (CH10) was selected for excavation. This trench did not yield any remains. The main area selected for excavation seems to have a maximum number of burials. As many as 70 burials/burial pits have been discovered in an area measuring over 35 × 21 m (735 m2). Trench CE2 was excavated in the year of 2007-08 (Fig. 1.5).

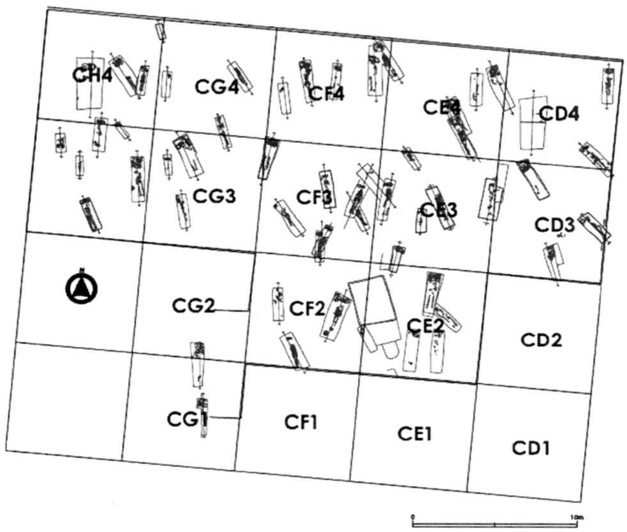

Figure 1.5: Trench map of excavation in 2008-09

The burials found at Farmana can be divided into three categories, i.e. primary (Fig. 1.6), secondary (Fig. 1.7) and symbolic (Fig. 1.8). In case of the primary burial, the dead body was placed in a pit in a supine position with head towards the north and the legs towards the south. The primary burial, therefore, contains full skeleton in situ. The secondary burial usually contains few bones. It is quite likely that the dead body was buried for some time and later survived bones were collected and buried in a pit ceremoniously. There

Figure 1.6: Primary burial at Farmana

Figure 1.7: Secondary burial at Farmana

Figure 1.8: Symbolic burial at Farmana

are some burials which are devoid of any skeletal remains but contained pottery and/or ornaments. Such burials have been termed as symbolic burial. It is quite likely that the body of the person was not retrieved but they thought it befitting to give ceremonious burial without the dead body or it is a part of burial custom. All the burial pits, excavated so far, are of the human life-size and rectangular in shape with their sides cut perfectly vertical and the bottom flat. This has been the hallmark of the site of Farmana, as all the small pits, including fire-pits, no matter whether they are connected with the burial or habitation activity, are usually rectangular in shape. The number of pots and jewelry found in burial pits varied from burial to burial, depending possibly on the social and economic status of the individual. The presence of burial goods clearly suggests that the Harappans believed in life after death. Detailed documentation on cultural and archaeological aspects of burials from Farmana is given in earlier publication (Shinde *et al* 2009 and 2011).

2

Necropolis at Farmana and Methodology of Analysis

This section briefly discusses the archaeological information on the burials and the material which was available for anthropological analysis. Further, it describes the methodology adopted for the study. Some observations are conducted on the taphonomical changes in human skeletal remains. Some skeletons were extremely fragile to lift from the site. So some long bone measurements were taken on the site itself. The field photographs of each skeleton provided for reference. Following table gives details about a number of specimens lifted from the field and reached to anthropology lab: (abbreviations: P= primary, SE: secondary, SY: symbolic, UN: unidentified, NA: not available) (Table 2.1).

Table 2.1: Burials from Farmana

Burial no	Material Available in the lab	Burial type	Period	Comments	Field photograph
1	Yes	P	NA	Excavated in 2006-07	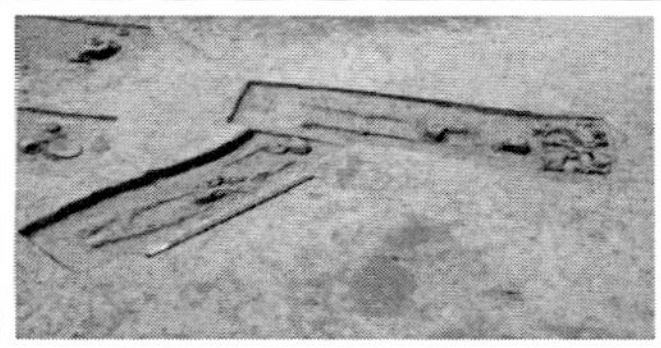
2	Yes	P	NA	Excavated in 2006-07	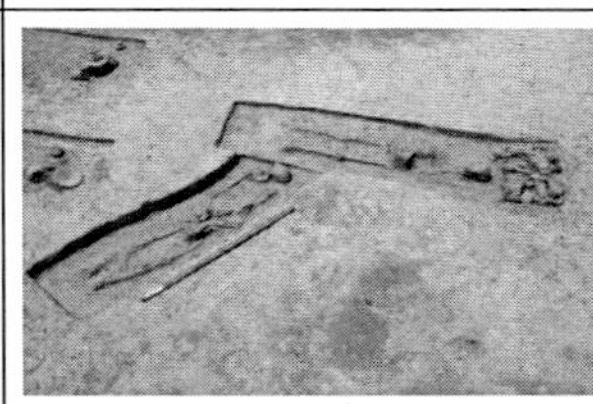
3	Yes	SE/P*	NA	Excavated in 2006-07	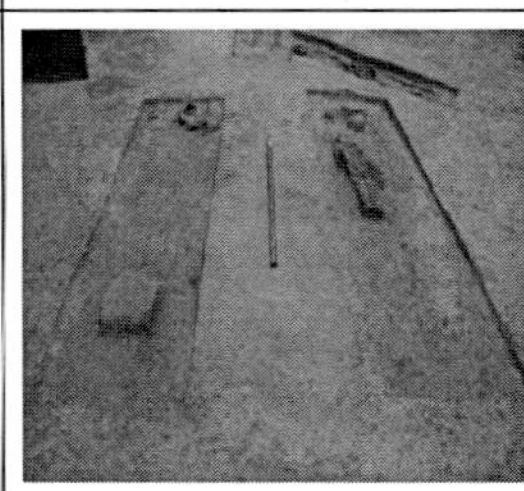
4	No	SE	NA	Excavated in 2006-07	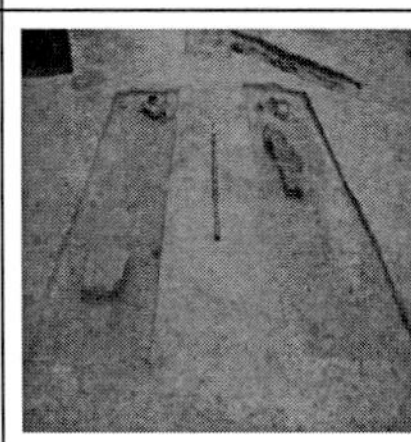

Burial no	Material Available in the lab	Burial type	Period	Comments	Field photograph
5	Yes	SE/P*	NA	Excavated in 2006-07	
6	Yes	SE/P*	NA	Excavated in 2006-07	
7	No	SY	NA	Excavated in 2006-07	-
8	Yes	P	IIC		
9	No	-	UN	Not excavated	-
10	Yes	P	IIC		
11	Yes	P	IIC		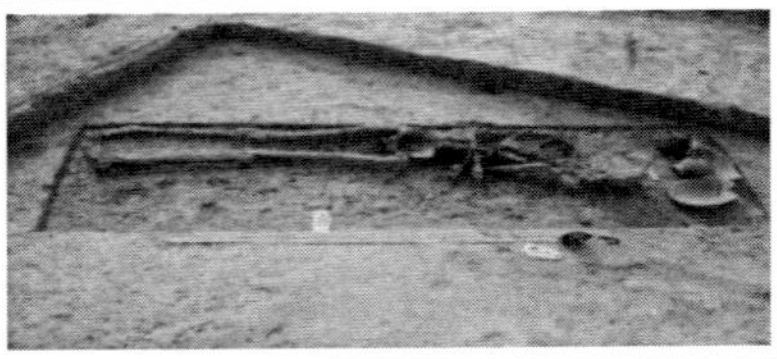
12	No	SY	IIB		

Burial no	Material Available in the lab	Burial type	Period	Comments	Field photograph
13	No	SE?	-	Not lifted	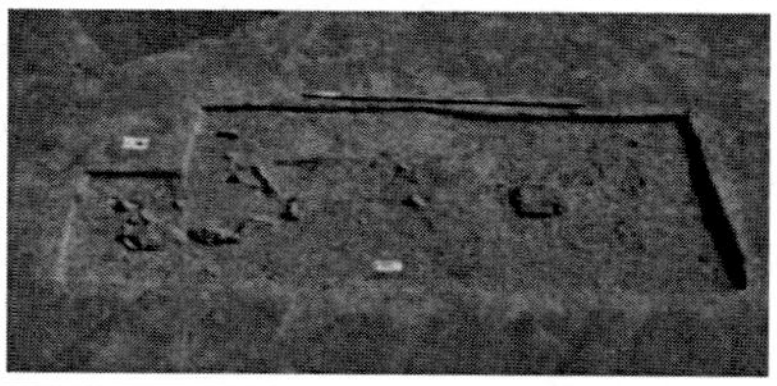
14	Yes	P	IIB		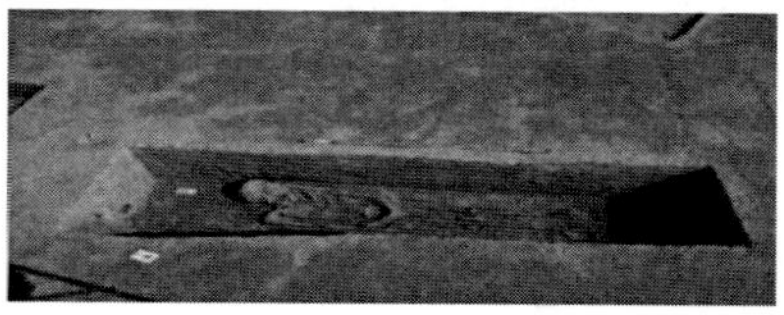
15	Yes	P	IIC		
16	No	SE?	IIC	Not lifted	
17	No	SY	IIC		
18	Yes	P	IIC		
19	No	SY?	IIC		
20	Yes	P	IIC		

Burial no	Material Available in the lab	Burial type	Period	Comments	Field photograph
21	No	P	IIB	Not lifted	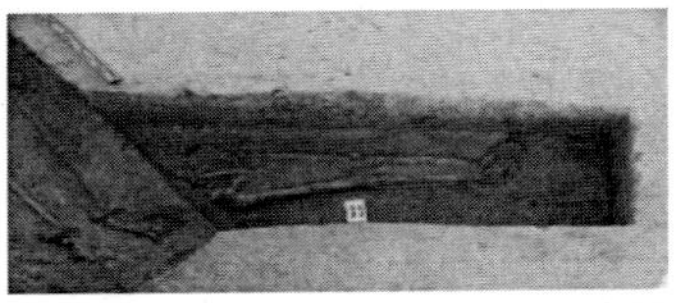
22	No	P	IIB	Not lifted	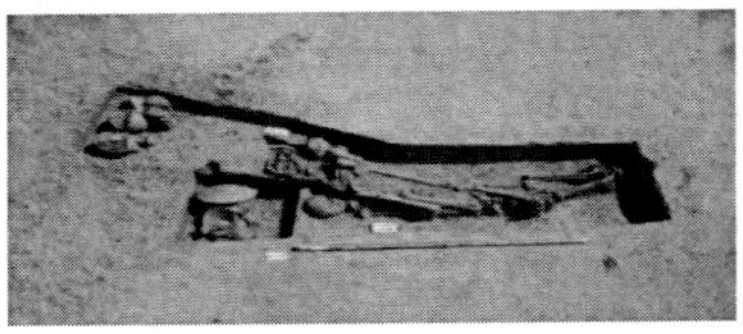
23	Yes	P	IIB		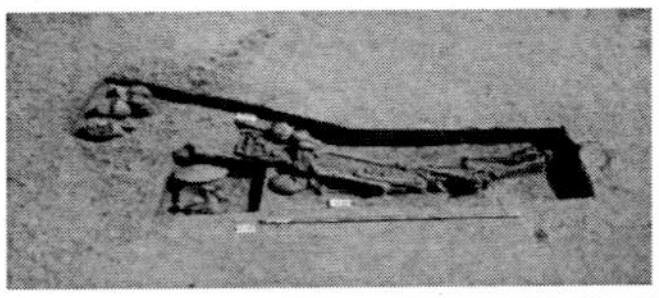
24	No	P	IIC	Not lifted	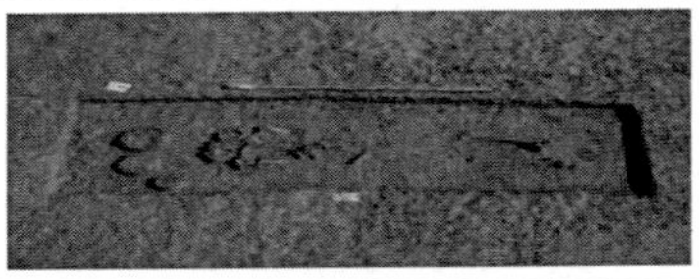
25	Yes	SE	IIC		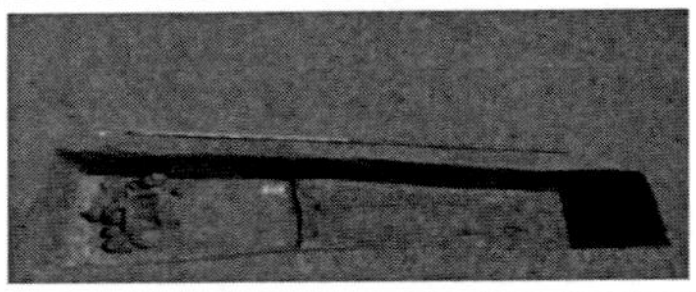
26	Yes	P	IIC		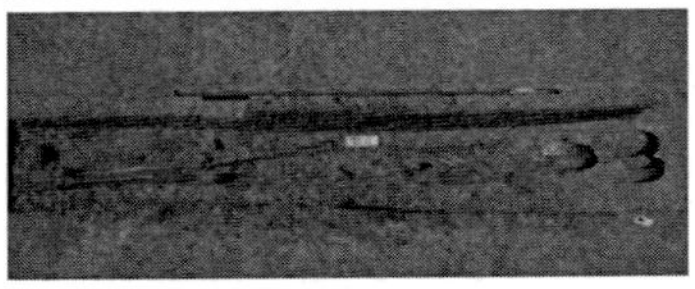
27	No	P?	IIA	Not lifted	
28	Yes	P	IIA		
29	No	SY	IIB		
30	No	-	UN	Not excavated	-

Burial no	Material Available in the lab	Burial type	Period	Comments	Field photograph
31	No	-	UN	Not excavated	-
32	Yes	P	IIA		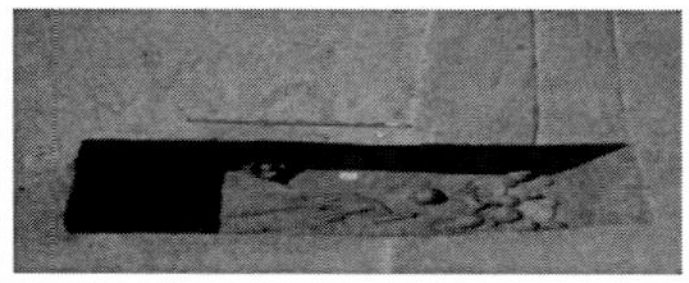
33	No	SY?	IIC		
34	Yes	SE	IIC		
35	No	P	IIC	Not lifted	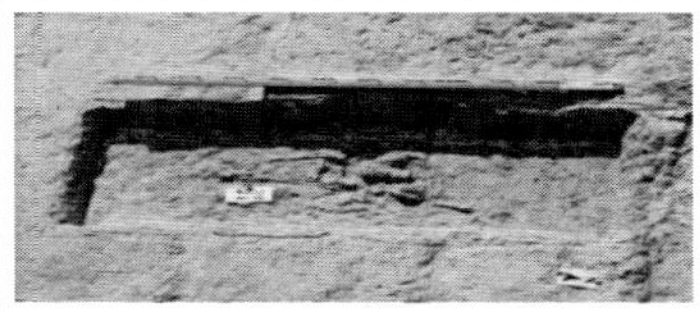
36	No	P	IIC	Not lifted	
37	No	-	UN	Not excavated	-
38	No	-	UN	Not excavated	-
39a	Yes	SE	IIB		
39b	Yes	SE	IIB		Same as above
40	No	P	IIA	Not lifted	
41	Yes	P	IIC		

Burial no	Material Available in the lab	Burial type	Period	Comments	Field photograph
42	No	SY	IIB		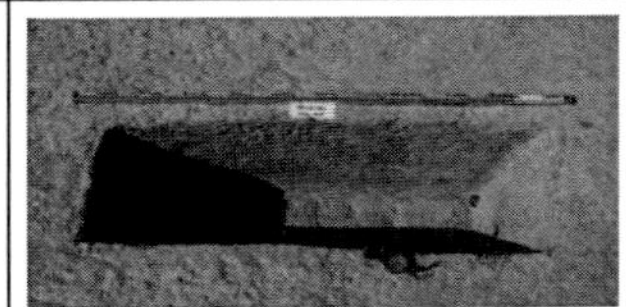
43	No	-	UN	Not excavated	-
44	No	SY	IIB		-
45	Yes	P	IIB		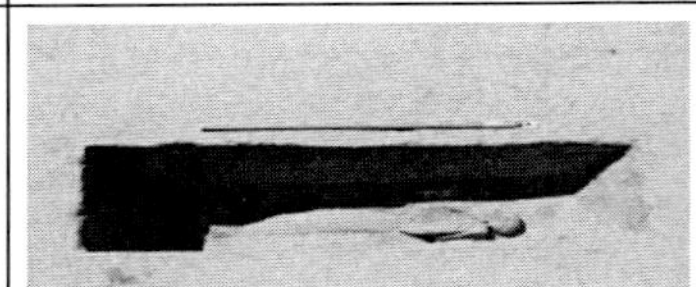
46	No	-	UN	Not excavated	-
47	Yes	SE	IIC		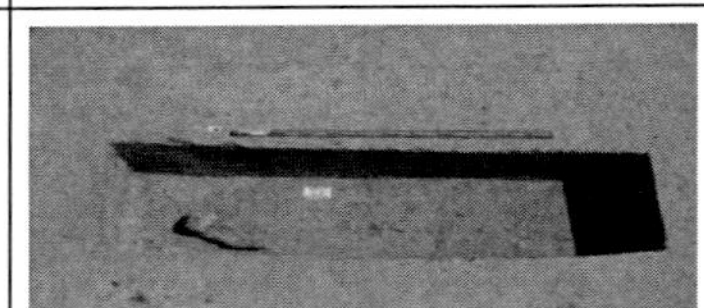
48	Yes	P	IIB		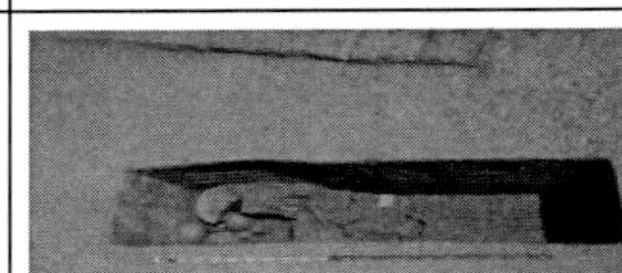
49	No	P?	IIB	Not lifted	
50a	Yes	P	IIB		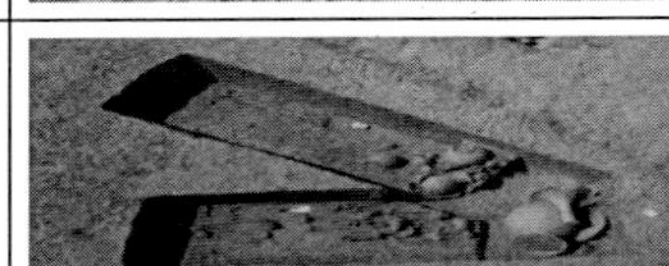
50b	Yes	P	IIB		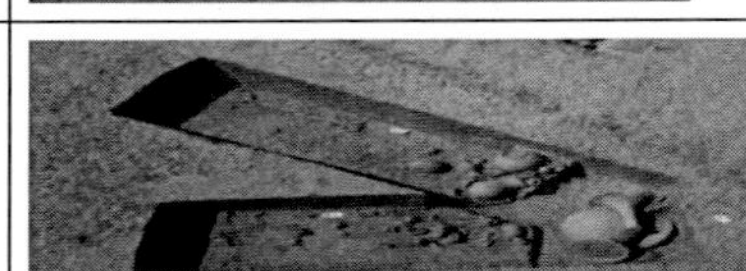
51	No	-	UN	Not excavated	-
52	Yes	SE?	IIC		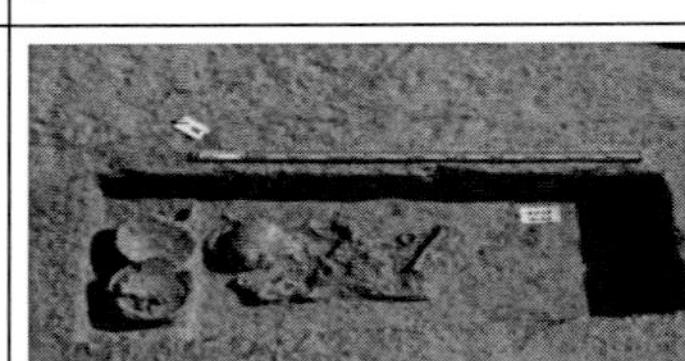

Burial no	Material Available in the lab	Burial type	Period	Comments	Field photograph
53	Yes	P	IIC		
54	Yes	P	IIB		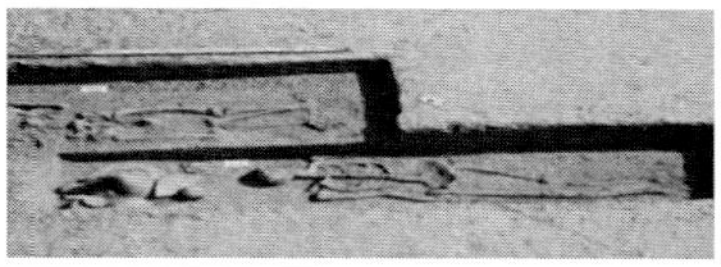
55	No	SE	IIB	Not lifted	
56	No	SE	IIA	Not lifted	
57	No	-	UN	Not excavated	-
58	Yes	SE	IIB		
59	No	-	UN	Not excavated	-
60	No	SY	IIC		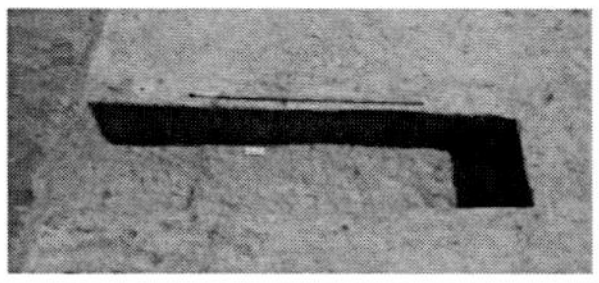
61	No	-	UN	Not excavated	-
62	Yes	P	IIC		
63	No	-	UN	Not excavated	-
64	Yes	P	IIC		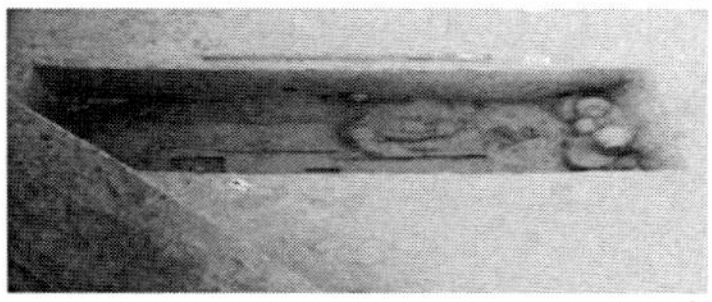

Burial no	Material Available in the lab	Burial type	Period	Comments	Field photograph
65	Yes	P	IIC		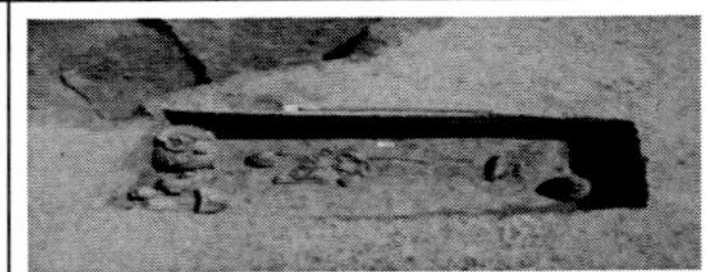
66	Yes	SE	IIC		
67	Yes	P	IIC		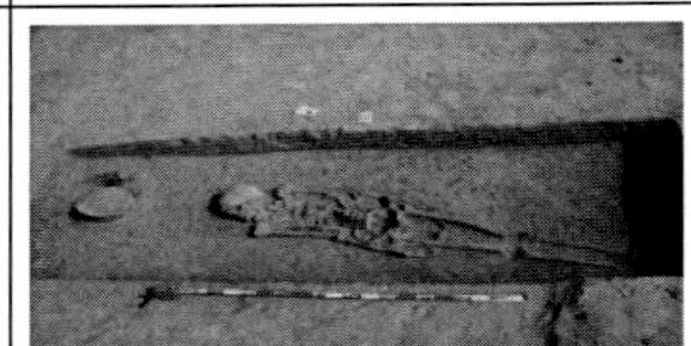
68	No	SE?	IIA	Not lifted	
69	No	-	UN	Not excavated	-
70	No	SY	IIC		

*Probably primary burial instead of secondary burial

As one can see total 70 burial pits were marked in the site out of which 58 were excavated consecutively for two years, 2007-08 and 2008-2009 seasons. In 2007-08 total 7 burials were excavated and skeletal remains from 5 pits came to the anthropology laboratory. In 2008-09, total 51 pits were excavated and the skeletal remains from 29 burials were available for analysis. Out of marked burials from the cemetery, 13 burials were not excavated and 10 symbolic burials were identified. The skeletal material from 12 burials (7 primary and 5 secondary burials) was not lifted from the field. In total 35 individuals were reached in the lab for analysis (Table 2.2).

Table 2.2: Period wise distribution of the burials

Period	No. of burials excavated	Available material in the lab (specimen numbers are in bracket)
Burials from 2007-08 excavation	7	5 (1,2,3,5 and 6)
Period IIA	6	2 (28 and 32)
Period IIB	18	10 (14, 23, 39a, 39b, 45, 48, 50a, 50b, 54 and 58)
Period IIC	27	18 (8, 10, 11, 15, 18, 20, 25, 26, 34, 41, 47, 52, 53, 62, 64, 65, 66 and 67)

There are certain limitations encountered while conducting the research on this material. It is very important to note that taphonomical changes limited the scope of the analysis. Preservation of the skeletal elements is far from satisfaction. There are many burials which were exposed in the field but bones could not reached lab because of poor preservation. Few possible measurements and observations were carried out in the field itself and pits were again filled with soil.

The cemetery is part of the present cultivation land. There are furrow marks observed on the ground and burials which were closer to the present surface got damaged by agricultural activities (Fig. 2.1). Soil at the cemetery was not conducive for the preservation of bones. Excavated remains overexposed to natural elements which further damaged them. Most of the preserved parts belong to skull portions and shaft region of long bones. Extremities of long bones, ribs, vertebrae, pelvis and other small bones are almost absent and even though they are present, they are in the clay lumps or extremely fragmented. For some individuals teeth are also damaged. In certain incidences, the skull mould is preserved and cranial bones are disintegrated (Fig. 2.2).

Figure 2.1: Furrow marks right on the burial

Figure 2.2: Skull mould without any bones attached to it

The burial no. 52 is a primary burial which was previously thought of secondary burial. The depth of the pit was 20 cm. This child burial have a skull, ribs, part of the humerus, both radii, and femur. Three pots were found with its primary position. At first glance, bones looked disarticulated and without any orientation. But after close observation, it indicated that the disturbance was due to agricultural activity (Fig. 2.3). The burial pit was shallow in the present context but probably it was deep at the time of burying the child. During the cleaning of the cranium, charred seeds were noticed below the occipital bone under fragile and damaged nuchal crest where the soil was softer than the other area (Fig. 2.4). They occurred mainly on the surface but in some areas, it was found almost 0.5-1.00 cm inside. The charred seeds perhaps accumulated due to the water percolation process. These were meticulously collected for botanical analysis and send to the Palaeobotanical Laboratory for identification. They were identified as seeds of *Asphodelus fistulosus* L., a member of the Liliaceae family (Presently Asphodelaceae Family) commonly known as onion weed, onion-leafed asphodel and pink asphodel (Dr. Satish Naik, *personal communication*). The antiquity of the seeds is questionable and yet to be dated. They were found on the left side of crania which was resting on the burial floor where water probably getting accumulated.

Figure 2.3: Post burial disturbance in burial pit

Figure 2.4: Charred seeds below the cranial bones

In the case of burial 25 (Fig. 2.5), only the lower extremity including femur and tibia belonging to both sides are present. It either indicates that the person died somewhere else and later got buried in the cemetery or another possibility that rest of bones are disintegrated without a trace, which seems to be impossible. This is most likely reflect the different burial practice at Farmana. In one large burial pit of burial 58, only one bone fragment was recovered and it was extremely fragile (Fig. 2.6).

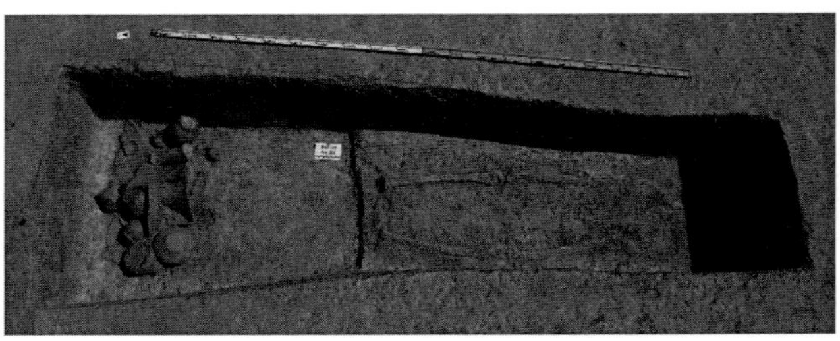

Figure 2.5: Secondary burial or non-survival of bones

Figure 2.6: Extremely fragile bone fragment in large burial pit

As this is agricultural land, bioturbation such as rodent and root activities were observed. This resulted in displacement of skeletal parts within the burial pits.

Methodology

The study is conducted following the standard and universally accepted methodologies. Major book references are given below. For very specific observations or studies, the methodologies are given at the point where they are mentioned.

- Determination of age and sex: Brothwell (1981), Olivier (1969), Stewart (1979), Buikstra and Ubelaker (1994) and Louise Scheuer and Sue Black OBE (2004)
- Assessment of morphological features: Buikstra and Ubelaker (1994), Steckel and Rose (2002).
- Metric analysis: Martin-Saller (1957).
- Stature estimation: Trotter (1970) formulae for White populations.

- Odontometry: Moorrees (1957a, 1957b), Wolpoff (1971), Potter *et al.* (1981), Dahlberg (1963).
- Dental morphology: Turner II *et al.* (1991).
- Pathological observations and interpretation: Larsen (1997), Ortner and Putschar (2003), Roberts and Manchester (2010), and Lukacs (1989).

Craniometric and osteometric methods used in this report follow Martin and Saller (1957). All the measurements, unless otherwise specified, are in millimeters. Cases where the reading is an estimated guess, the measurement is recorded in the bracket. Stature estimation, using complete and intact long bones, follow the method of Trotter (1970), where racially specific equations for White populations are used. Currently there are no standard available for South Asian population for stature therefore the stature estimation was conducted using Trotter's formula.

Assessment of non-metric discrete cranial and post-cranial traits (minor variants) is attempted using a standardized coding system of Ubelaker and Buikstra (1994). These traits are described and analyzed for population comparisons. As noted by many researchers, an advantage of non-metric traits is the fact that they may be recorded in fragmentary, incomplete, and poorly preserved materials.

Two basic measurements have been carried out for each tooth following the Moorrees' (1957a, 1957b) technique. These consist of maximum crown length (mesio-distal diameter) and maximum crown breadth (bucco-lingual diameter). The mesio-distal diameter (MD) is the maximum dimension of the tooth crown in the mesio-distal direction, parallel to the occlusal and the labial surface. The bucco-lingual crown diameter (BL) is defined as the greatest distance between the buccal and the lingual surface of tooth crown in a plane perpendicular to that of the mesio-distal diameter. The crown measurements are carried out with electronic MAX-CAL digital calliper with an accuracy of 0.01 mm.

The primary comparative standard in the analysis of tooth size is the crown area (CA) or the cross-sectional area of the tooth. This figure of crown size is obtained by multiplying mesio-distal diameter by bucco-lingual diameter. The crown index (CI), a measure of crown shape is the ratio of mesio-distal and bucco-lingual diameter expressed in terms of percentage, as suggested by Wolpoff (1971). The measure of crown bulk, crown module (CM), is the average of mesio-distal and bucco-lingual values.

Specific observations of dental morphology have been made on maxillary and mandibular permanent dentition. The observations are made on undamaged and unworn teeth. Most of the archaeological permanent dental elements exhibit considerable attrition resulting in partial or complete obliteration of occlusal features, so not all teeth could be studied.

The structural variations observed on permanent teeth include the following:

Maxillary Dentition

- Shovel Shaping of Incisor
- Metacone size variation in molars
- Hypocone size variation in molars
- Cusp 5 (metaconule) size variation in molars
- Carabelli's trait in molars
- Para style cusp variation in molars

Mandibular Dentition

- Groove pattern in molars

- Molar cusp number
- Cusp 5 (hypoconulid) size variation
- Cusp 6 (entonconulid) size variation
- Cusp 7 (metaconulid) size variation

The comparisons on the basis of dental morphology have several limitations owing to the lack of common methodology. Expression of dental traits, discrete or continuous, often lead to certain arbitrariness and also the methods used in evaluating the expression of certain dental variables vary greatly. In the present study, the assessment of morphological variations has been attempted using reference plaster plaques prepared by the ASU Dental Anthropology System (Turner II. *et al.* 1991).

The palaeopathological investigation is a recent development in the field of human skeletal biology in India. It deals with the skeletal pathologies and anomalies in the light of ecology, environmental changes, subsistence pattern and social organization giving bio-cultural perspective. Differences in status and rank are expected to have effects on health and nutrition of people because of differential access to the food resources. These health and dietary differences are reflected in the bones and can be studied in archaeological populations.

The methods of study in palaeopathology are many, but at the primary level usually, rely on macroscopic observation. Tools like radiography, stable isotopic studies, scanning electron microscopy, help accurate diagnosis of the lesion (Roberts and Manchester 2010). The following are the broad categories considered for palaeopathological observations;

Infectious disease: caused by invading living organisms (viruses, bacteria etc.)

Traumatic lesions: caused by injury or malformation of the skeleton and associated soft tissue

Joint disease: diseases that affect the joints of the body and their associated soft tissue

Metabolic disease: caused by a disturbance in the normal process of cell metabolism

Neoplastic or new bone formation: it is malignant or progressive growth which invades and destroys surrounding tissues and spread to more distant sites in the body beneath the skin

Stress factors: they are indicators of the repetitive use of one part of the body resulting in bone remoulding

Dental disease: it covers dental anomalies like caries, enamel hypoplasia etc.

3

Inventory of Skeletal Remains

This part gives information about individual-wise inventory. This is one of the important stage of analysis. Table 3.1 provide what parts are preserved for each individual.

Table 3.1: Inventory of skeletal elements from the site

Specimen No	Skull	Dentition	Thoracic Cage	Upper Extremity	Lower Extremity
1	Cranial fragments including one big fragment of L and two medium fragments of R parietal bone, one big fragment of occipital, one small fragment of R temporal, around 15 chips of more than 5mm bones and around 20 chips of less than 5 mm	**Maxilla**: LM3 (isolated broken fragment)	-	**Humerus:** L 7 medium sized fragments of shaft and distal end, extremely damage, olecranon fossa and partly preserved epicondyles. Around 4 small fragments of either of ulna or radial shaft, individual or side identification not possible.	**Femur:** R Three big fragments of proximal end, distal end and part of distal shaft present with 6 small to medium fragments of femoral head, partly preserved neck, greater trochanter and medial condyle, extremely fragile; L one big and one medium badly preserved fragment of femoral shaft, both extremities are broken and missing. **Patella:** R complete but damaged. **Tibia**: R two big and 3 medium fragments of proximal end, shaft and portion of distal end. Extremely damage bones; L 5 medium fragments of proximal end, distal end and shaft present, extremely damage condition. Around 30 small to medium chips of tibia and fibula. **Phalange:** R 1st row phalange preserved into two pieces, extremely damage in condition. Around 50 long bone chips unidentified.

Specimen No	Skull	Dentition	Thoracic Cage	Upper Extremity	Lower Extremity
2	Cranial bones almost preserved, extremely damaged L frontal portion, partially preserved facial bones, partially preserved nasal bones; L zygomatic bones are broken and missing. Maxilla not well preserved and bones missing in many areas. Almost complete but damaged mandible attached to the skull **(Fig. 3.1 to 3.4)**	**Maxilla**: RLI1, RLI2, RLC, RLPm1, RLPm2, RLM1, RLM2, RLM3, present *in situ*. **Mandible**: RLI1, RLI2, RLC, PLPm1, RLPm2, RLM1, RLM2, RLM3, present *in situ*. Samples for isotope analysis has been taken from mandibular LM1,2,3.	Damaged ribs are present. Highly damaged axis, atlas and probably two cervical vertebrae with the skull, individual identification is not possible.	-	-
3.	Endocast retaining the shape of the skull cap with right temporal bone attached on it **(Fig. 3.5 and 3.6)**. Traces of foramen magnum, isolated fragments include frontal bone with portion of left orbital border, 12 medium and around 15 small fragments of frontal, temporal and occipital bones.	-	-	-	**Femur**: L distal end with part of medial condyle, lateral condyle missing. Distal portion of shaft present, patellar area damaged, extremely poor condition of preservation. **Tibia:** two medium sized fragile fragments of shaft, side identification not possible.
5	Portion having endocast of parietal and occipital area, distorted shape and containing few skull pieces of parietal and occipital. Individual identification is not possible.	**Maxilla**: Rdm2 (isolated and root broken). Dental cast of Rdm1is present.	A soil blocks containing a small fragment of ribs. Extremely damage condition.	**Humerus**: R two medium and one small fragments of almost entire shaft and portion of lateral condyle present **(Fig. 3.7)**. poor condition	**Femur:** R probably a medial side of distal end, extremely damage and fragile. Exact identification not possible. Around 25 small to medium long bone fragile fragment unidentified.
6	Complete mandible present, moderately preserved. L condyle and R coronoid partly broken, chin area and alveolar process above chin area partly broken. **(Fig. 3.8)**	**Mandible**: RC (root *in situ,*), LPm1 (root *in situ*), LPm2 (root *in situ*), LM1 (root and part of dentine present *in situ* and broken crown isolated), LM2 (root and part of dentine present in situ), LM3 (slightly broken *in situ*). Parts of LM1, LM2 and LM3 taken for isotope analysis.	-	**Humerus:** L almost complete head and portion of proximal shaft present in two separate fragments, moderate preserved. Trochlea well preserved, both epicondyles are partly broken, olecranon fossa partly broken. Around 15 small and 1 medium fragments are also present.	-

Specimen No	Skull	Dentition	Thoracic Cage	Upper Extremity	Lower Extremity
8	-	-	-	-	**Pelvic**: Fragment of an extremely damage body of right pelvic with broken sciatic notch and portion of acetabulam. **Femur:** R preset in fragments, shaft preserved in 2 large and 2 medium fragments, one head fragments extremely fragile, **Patella:** R attached to the distal end of R femur, extremely damaged. **Tibia:** R almost complete bone, part of proximal and distal ends missing. Bone preservation on the posterior surface is very poor. One long bone chip present
10	-	-	Around 5 small to medium fragments of mid shaft of ribs, extremely damage and fragile.	**Humerus:** R 2 big fragments of distal end and shaft and around 10 small to medium fragments present, upper portion of olecranon fossa preserved; L one big fragment of shaft and three medium damaged fragments. Both extremities missing. **Ulna:** R an extremely damage olecranon process, one large ulnar shaft and around 5 small bone chips, extremely damage and side unidentified. **Radius:** one big and two small damaged fragment of shaft, side unidentified. **Carpal bones:** R extremely damage and highly fragile, fragments of Hamate, Capitate, Naviculater, Greater and Lesser Maltangular present.	**Pelvis:** extremely fragile fragments of pelvic bones coming from both sides. Individual identification not possible. **Femur:** R extremely fragile shaft with partly preserved greater and lesser trochantor. **Tibia:** R extremely damaged shaft, few tiny bone chips; L extremely damage three big and one small fragments extremities and portion of shaft present **(Fig.3.9)**. **Fibula:** R one big and three small fragile fragments of shaft; L around 15 small to medium extremely damage shaft fragments

Specimen No	Skull	Dentition	Thoracic Cage	Upper Extremity	Lower Extremity
				Meta Carpal Bones: R complete 4th metacarpal (broken into two parts), two proximal ends with portion of shaft and three distal ends. Extremely fragile. **Phalanges:** R 5 first row phalanges, 3 second row phalanges, 3 third row phalanges and two unidentified phalanges.	**Tarsal bones:** R a block of soil containing few tarsal bones, extremely fragile, Separation and individual identification not possible. Around 20 small to medium long bone chips.
11	**Mandible**: one fragment of chin portion and one small fragment of R horizontal ramus present. Extremely damage and fragile in condition. **(Fig. 3.10)**	**Mandible**: LM2 (isolated broken crown, root present *in situ*) LM3 (isolated broken crown with part of root). Sample was taken isotope analysis from both the teeth.	-	-	-
14	Almost complete skull **(Fig. 3.11 to 3.14)**, damaged near left frontal, parietal and partially preserved occipital, foramen magnum present, R mastoid process present and L broken and missing, orbital borders are damaged, nasal bones are partly preserve, maxilla extremely damaged and not present in many places, maxillary cast retains the teeth *in situ,* Mandible attached to the skull, but damaged surface, RL condylar process damaged, RL horizontal ramus damage, chin portion partly preserve.	**Maxilla:** RI1, RI2, RC, RPm1, RPm2, LPm2, LM1, LM2 *in situ*. LI1 (isolated root fragment), LI2 (Isolated intact crown and broken root), LC (complete isolated), LPm1 (Isolated complete crown with broken root), RM1 (isolated broken portion of crown), RM3 (Isolated broken portion of crown). Samples for isotope analysis were taken from both RM1 and RM3, LM2 was probably sampled. **Mandible:** LC, LPm1, LPm2, LM1, LM2, RLM3 *in situ*. RLI1, RI2 and RM1 isolated. Three root and three crown fragments.	Soil block containing few thoracic vertebrae partially preserved but extremely damaged rib cage, individual identification not possible.	**Humerus:** R extremely damaged both ends; L shaft preserved in four fragments, both extremities missing.	**Femur:** R preserved in 3 fragments one with fragile proximal extremity with partially broken greater trochanter and neck, shaft fragment and third of distal shaft without condyles; L extremely fragile and fragmented but attached with soil, almost complete shaft, damaged distal end preserved in three fragments. **Tibia:** R severely damaged but almost complete shaft, preserved in four fragments; L almost complete with extremely damaged bone surface, both the extremities are highly damaged, preserved in two fragments. 50 small to medium long bone chips.
15	Only compressed endocast retaining the shape of the skull **(Fig. 3.15)** and only traces of bones attached on it. There are traces of eye socket, nasal bones and maxilla.	**Maxilla**: RLM1 isolated crown (developing stage). Fragment of anterior tooth crown probably of I1/I2, individual identification not possible.	-	-	-

Specimen No	Skull	Dentition	Thoracic Cage	Upper Extremity	Lower Extremity
18	Almost complete crania present with well preserved frontal, parietal and occipital bone **(Fig. 3.16 to 3.20)**, L temporal bone partly damage, R mastoid process partly damaged, foramen magnum present but partly damaged, well preserved facial bones with partly damaged nasal and extremely damaged maxilla but cast retains teeth *in situ*, mandible in two big fragments, extremely damage RL vertical and horizontal ramus, RL condyels partly preserve, chin portion extremely damage and isolated. Around 20 small chips of mandibular fragments.	**Maxilla:** RI1, RLI2, RLC, RLPm1, RLPm2, RLM1, RLM2 and RM3 present *in situ*, RM2 partly broken and only portion of crown present on the lingual side. Sample for isotope analysis. Root of LI1 is present. **Mandible:** RLPm2 (intact and attached two mandibular fragments) LM1 (root and portion of dentine present), RM2 (intact), LM2 (only root), RM3 (partly broken), LM3 (root) *in situ*, RM3 and LM2 has been taken for isotope analysis.	-	-	-
20	Complete skull present **(Fig. 3.21 to 3.24)**. Both mastoid processes are partly broken. L zygomatic arch and portion near glabella partly broken. *Norma basalaris* not visible. From facial region, R orbit preserved better than the L one. Nasal bones are extremely damage. R zygomatic bone and maxilla preserved better than the L. Mandible intact attached to the skull, except partly broken chin area. A thick layer of favicol has been applied to preserve the specimen.	All teeth of maxilla and mandible are present *in situ*, except RM1 and RM3, which has been taken for isotope analysis and the caste of RM3 is present.	Axis, atlas and probably 2 cervical vertebrae attached to the skull, individual identification not possible.	**Clavicle**: R into two pieces, almost complete except sternal end; L 2 fragments mid-shaft and lateral end present, sternum end missing. **Scapula**: R broken parts of acromion process, coracoid process and axillary border present. Extremely poor condition of preservation; L medium fragment of acromion process, one medium fragment of vertebral border, extremely damage. **Humerus**: R almost complete but in two fragments, one is head with part of shaft and other fragment of partial	**Femur**: R distal half with part of shaft and intact condyles. Moderate mode of preservation, L distal half with part of shaft and intact medial condyle. Moderate mode of preservation. **Patella**: R and L completely preserved but fragile with thick layer of favicol. **Tibia**: R preserved into three fragments, one of proximal end with part of upper extremity and another fragment of mid shaft region, distal end broken and present in the block containing foot bone, extremely damage and fragile

Specimen No	Skull	Dentition	Thoracic Cage	Upper Extremity	Lower Extremity
				shaft with distal end. Both the epicondyles are present. Extremely poor condition; L one big fragment comprising shaft and distal end, upper extremity broken and missing, well preserved condyles and trochlea. Preservation better than the right one. **Radius**: R preserved in 2 fragments, upper extremity with portion of shaft attached to distal end of humerus and the other fragment comprising the shaft with distal end broken; L proximal extremity present and attached to the distal end of humerus. **Ulna**: R preserved in two fragments, first is of proximal extremity with portion of upper shaft attached in the olecranon process of humerus. Other fragment isolated shaft, distal extremity broken and missing; L a medium fragment of upper extremity with portion of shaft attached to the olecronon fossa of humerus. **Metacarpals**: 2nd: proximal half probably of 2nd metacarpal. Extremely damaged.	in condition; L almost entire bone except the portion of distal extremity with poor preservation **Fibula**: R preserved in two pieces, small fragment of proximal end and big one of shaft. Distal end broken and present in the block containing foot bones, moderately preserved; L extremely damage and fragile fibular shaft present, both extremities broken and missing. **Tarsal, metatarsal and phalanges**: R a block of soil containing these bones, extremely damaged and fragile. Removal of individual bone is not possible. L only the traces of upper surface of bone present on the favicol layer, below it extremely fragile bones. Unidentified: around 50 small to medium fragments
23	Endocast retaining the shape of the crania and only a few traces of bones attached on it **(Fig. 3.25 to 3.28)**. Part of frontal bone near L orbital suture present. Around 60 isolated pieces of frontal, parietal, temporal and occipital present, part of zygomatic arch present. Facial	**Maxilla**: RLI1, RLI2, RLC, RLPm1, RLPm2, RLM1 present *in situ*, RLM2, probably present but not visible. **Mandible**: LC, LPm1, LPm2, LM1, LM2, present *in situ*. RM1, RM2 (isolated broken crown, taken for isotope analysis). RM3 was present but missing and			

Specimen No	Skull	Dentition	Thoracic Cage	Upper Extremity	Lower Extremity
	bones attached to the endocast, L orbit is present, R orbital socket extremely damage with traces of lateral, medial and lower border. Nasal bones are extremely damage with traces on the cast. L zygomatic bone and maxilla better present than the R side. Mandible attached to the skull. Only left vertical ramus and partly damage condyle, coronoid process and part of horizontal ramus present. On the other places cast retaining the shape.	only photograph is available	-	-	-
25	-	-	-	-	**Femur:** R preserved into one big and one small fragment, bone surface extremely damaged; L preserved into one big and one small fragment, small fragment comprising neck, greater and lesser trochantor, bone surface extremely damage but better preserved than the right one. **Tibia:** R almost complete tibia preserved into two fragments **(Fig. 3.29)**, one big and another medium, bone surface partly damage. Around 30 small to medium long bone chips.
26	Cranium comprising portion of frontal, three large fragments of parietal, occipital and temporal, RL zygomatic arches present, R mastoid process partly preserved, *Norma basalaris* partly preserved with traces of foramen magnum.	**Maxilla**: Pm2 (isolated intact, side identification not possible), LM3 (isolated crown), root of LRM3 and RM2 present *in situ,* two big and 8 small fragments of crown unidentified.	Broken fragment of isolated atlas, extremely fragile.		

Specimen No	Skull	Dentition	Thoracic Cage	Upper Extremity	Lower Extremity
	Mainly endocast retaining the shape of the skull and cranial bone fragments are attached in to it. Bone surface is extremely damage. From facial part, R orbital border partly present while the L almost present, nasal bones are extremely damage and fragile and only traces of it seen on the caste. R zygomatic bone almost missing and only cast retaining the shape, left one is better present. Maxillary bones severely damage and only traces present on the skull, portion of extremely damage palate present **(Fig. 3.30 to 3.34)**. Around 42 small to medium fragments of skull bone chips.			-	-
28	Endocast retaining the shape of the skull cap and contains fragment of extremely damage skull bones.	-	-	-	-
32	Crania comprising part of frontal, parietal and occipital bones **(Fig. 3.35 to 3.38)**. *Norma basalaris* not preserved but traces of bones and foramen magnum present on the endocast. Bone surface preserved well but the lateral side of frontal bone is broken and missing. L mastoid process is partly broken. From face, partly broken RL upper orbital border, L one better preserved, L lateral orbital border and L side nasal bone. Around 4 medium and 20 small fragments of skull.	-	Block of soil containing 5 lumbar, 3 thoracic vertebrae with 8 left ribs and 5 right ribs **(Fig. 3.39)**, and another block containing extremely damage upper body of sacrum. The condition of bone is very poor and individual identification not possible.	**Humerus:** L distal portion, olecranon fossa and medial epicondyle partly preserved. Lateral epicondyle broken and missing. Distal end of the shaft present, bone surface preserved moderately. **Ulna:** L only the proximal end with olecranon process is present. Around 8 small to medium long bone fragments.	**Pelvis**: Block of soil containing highly damage pelvic bone and acetabulum **Femur:** R complete bone moderately preserved; L distal end present with condyels and distal portion of shaft preserved. Extremely damaged bone surface. **Patella:** L present. **Tibia:** R almost entire bone except, proximal end, L entire bone present with moderately preserved bone surface. **Fibula:** R portion of proximal end, distal end and mid-shaft attached to the right tibia in to three parts; L both proximal and distal end attached to

Specimen No	Skull	Dentition	Thoracic Cage	Upper Extremity	Lower Extremity
					the left tibia, portion of mid-shaft isolated and broken into one big and another medium fragment. **Tarsal:** R calcaneus and talus present, preserved in a better condition; L talus present. **Metatarsals**: two metatarsal attached to the talus.
34	Cranial cap comprising part of frontal, parietal, temporal and occipital bone **(Fig. 3.40 to 3.42)**, L portion of frontal and parietal bones extremely damage than the R portion, L temporal bone better preserved than the R part, L mastoid process partly preserved, around 5 small unidentified chips are present.				
39A	Endocast retaining the shape of the crania and partially preserved L parietal, occipital, part of L temporal, glabella region and L part of frontal bones **(Fig. 3.43)** Around 47 small to medium fragments of skull chips, extremely damage and fragile in condition.	-	-	-	-
39B	Skull cap with part of frontal, temporal and occipital bone **(Fig. 3.44 to 3.46)**. Orbital borders present. There are two medium and around 15 small fragments of temporal and occipital bones present. Bones are thick and moderately well preserved. Left temporal line partly visible. Mandible preserved in two fragments, one big part of R horizontal ramus with part of vertical ramus and chin area and traces of root in it.	**Maxilla**: a longitudinal fragment of molar, individual identification not possible (Sample taken for isotope analysis) **Mandible**: a longitudinal fragment of molar, individual identification not possible (Sample taken for isotope analysis) Small fragments of roots and crowns.			

Specimen No	Skull	Dentition	Thoracic Cage	Upper Extremity	Lower Extremity
	Another medium fragment of horizontal ramus with traces of root and a small fragment of chin area. Extremely damage in condition.				
41	Fragment of endocast of skull and around 62 small to medium fragments of crania, extremely fragile.	**Maxilla**: RC (isolated crown), RM1 (isolated and labial part of crown), RLM2 (isolated crown) **Mandible**: RI2 (isolated crown)	-	-	-
45	Crania extremely fragile, damage portion of RL parietal and occipital present, traces of frontal and R temporal present, bones are attached to the endocast **(Fig. 3.47 to 3.50)**. From face region, partly preserved orbital border and nasal bone and traces of maxilla on the cast. R mandibular portion present, vertical ramus well preserved with partly preserved condoyle and extremely damage coronoid, part of horizontal ramus preserved.	**Maxilla**: RI2 (isolated and portion of maxilla attached into it), LC (isolated, intact with root), RPm1(isolated and longitudinally broken, taken for isotopic analysis) RPm2(isolated crown, root missing), RM1 (isolated tooth with partly broken root, intact crown), RM2 (isolated and portion of maxilla attached into it). One fragment of tooth, either maxillary incisor or canine, identification was not possible **Mandible**: RI1 and I2 (isolated but joined together and portion of mandible attached into it), RC (isolated, partly damage), RPm2 (isolated, intact crown, root present *in situ*), RM1-M2 (present in situ)	**Thoracic cage**: a block of soil containing around 4 thoracic, 5 lumbar vertebrae, 5 pair of ribs and extremely damage upper body of sacrum. Extremely fragile condition and individual identification is not possible.	**Scapula**: 6 extremely damaged small to medium fragments of glenoid cavity, spine near acromion process and body. **Humerus**: 2 large and around 7 small to medium fragments of shaft, extremely damage, side identification not possible. **Radius**: one distal end extremely damaged, side identification not possible.	
47	Endocast retaining the shape of the skull and traces of extremely thin and fragile fragments of frontal, parietal, temporal and occipital, 5 small fragments of skull chips, foramen magnum present, traces of L orbit, nasal bone and R zygomatic bone present, mainly cast retaining the shape.	**Maxilla**: RC (isolated crown with broken root), RPm1 (isolated crown with broken root), LPm2 (isolated crown with broken root), RPm2 (2 crown fragments) sample taken for isotope analysis. LM2 (Isolated crown) **Mandible**: LI2 (isolated tooth with broken root)	-	-	-

Specimen No	Skull	Dentition	Thoracic Cage	Upper Extremity	Lower Extremity
48	-	-	Three thoracic vertebrae, 5 lumbar and upper body of sacrum attached to each other. One small fragment of rib shaft is also present. The preservation is moderate.	**Clavicle:** a small fragment of medial shaft, extremely fragile, side unidentified. **Humerus:** R one big and one medium fragment of mid-shaft and distal shaft, both extremities missing. Extremely fragile; L two medium fragment of mid-shaft extremely fragile, one medium sized fragment unidentified.	**Femur:** R preserved into two big fragments of mid- shaft and distal end, anterior surface preserved better than the posterior surface; L 2 fragments, big sized of mid-shaft and one medium fragment of neck, attached to the cast, damage surface and anterior surface preserve better than the posterior surface. **Tibia:** R preserved into two medium fragments, preservation of proximal and distal end is very poor. Mainly cast retaining the shape and traces of bones; L preserved into four medium fragments of proximal end, mid-shaft and distal end. Extremely damage, mainly cast retaining the shape and traces of bones are attached into it. **Tarsal:** L fragment of bone attached to the distal end of left tibia. **Phalange:** L fragment of first phalange except the distal end is present, preservation is moderate. There are around 100 medium to small fragments unidentified.
50A	Crania comprising with big fragment of occipital bone with part of L temporal bone and a small fragment of L mastoid process with part of L temporal bone. Around 13 small to medium fragments of occipital and L temporal, moderately preserved.	-	-	-	-

Specimen No	Skull	Dentition	Thoracic Cage	Upper Extremity	Lower Extremity
50 B	-	-	An unidentified lumbar body part, extremely damaged sacrum body	**Humerus**: extremely damaged few parts including a broken head portion, one fragment of upper shaft with partially preserved deltoid tuberosity and three small portion of shaft, side identification not possible. **Radius**: comprising with three extremely damaged small portion of radial shaft, the side identification not possible. **Metacarpal**: broken, damaged distal end of metacarpal, side and number identification not possible.	**Pelvis**: bones are in the block of soil, extremely damaged RL iliac blades, R one better preserved. R sciatic notch preserved but partly damaged, isolated broken part of RL acetabulum is present, right better preserved. **Femur**: Extremely damaged head, one epiphysis fragment and a medium sized fragment of mid-shaft. Side identification not possible. **Fibula**: one small damaged fragment of shaft, side identification not possible. **Unidentified**: badly damaged two head portions and around 100 small to medium long bone chips.
52	Almost entire crania present, except occipital and part of left parietal. Traces of Zygomatic arch present. **(Fig. 3.51 to 3.53)** R temporal bone preserved better than the L one. Around 10 small fragments of skull present. From facial region RL orbits, L better preserved than the R one, orbital borders are damaged, traces of nasal bones on the endocast. Both RL zygomatic bones are present but extremely damaged and R preserved better than the L side. Maxilla almost broken but traces of roots present. Extremely damaged mandibular R vertical ramus attached with skull. Condyle and coronoid process present. One fragment of R horizontal	**Maxilla**: Ldi1 (complete but isolated), RLdm1 (isolated, root broken), Rdm2 (intact *in situ*), Ldm2(isolated, root broken) **Mandible**: LI2 (isolated, root broken), Rdc (complete, *in situ*), Rdm1 (isolated, root broken), Ldm2 (isolated, complete crown, route broken), Rdm2 (isolated partly broken crown and root), RI2 (partly complete crown calcification)	-	-	-

Specimen No	Skull	Dentition	Thoracic Cage	Upper Extremity	Lower Extremity
	ramus with portion of chin present. Traces of roots and RI2 present with this fragment.				
53	Cranial cap almost complete with frontal, parietal and occipital bones **(Fig. 3.54 to 3.56)**. Traces of L temporal present. Foramen magnum present, both mastoid process and zygomatic arch missing, R orbital border partly present but L almost broken. 7 small fragments of skulls are present. Facial bones are extremely fragile. L orbit partly present R present but extremely damage. Nasal bones are fragile and only traces present on the cast. R zygomatic bone present but damage and fragile, L one almost broken and only traces remain. Palate present but maxilla and mandible missing.	-	Block of soil contains 2nd and 3rd thoracic vertebra, and another containing 4th and 5th lumber vertebra and upper body of sacrum and both the pelvic bones, very poor preservation and individual identification was done on the in situ association with other bones.	-	Block of soil which contains 4th, 5th lumber vertebra and sacrum, also contains left pubic bone. Another block contains the right pelvic. **(Fig. 3.57)**. In both blocks bones of iliac crest present but pubic and ischium absent. R sciatic notch partly preserve.
54	Fragment of endocast, mainly the portion of occipital area, retaining the shape of the skull and containing traces of bones. A big fragment of parietal bone, two medium fragments of occipital bone and around 45 small to medium fragments of skull chips are present. Mandible present in three medium sized fragments including ramus and condoyle. One fragment containing traces of roots. Mainly cast retaining shape and traces of bones.	**Mandible**: RM1 (isolated broken crown), sample taken for isotope analysis.	-	-	Block of soil containing portion of sacrum and pelvic, extremely damage bones, 4 irregular shaped small bones unidentified.

Specimen No	Skull	Dentition	Thoracic Cage	Upper Extremity	Lower Extremity
58	Mandibular big fragment of R vertical ramus, two medium fragments of horizontal ramus with traces of root, one fragment of condyle and around 15 small fragments present. Mainly cast retaining the shape and extremely damage small fragments of bones.	**Mandible**: RM2 (isolated molar, broken crown, root missing) sample taken for isotope analysis and side determination is been done on the basis of available cast.	-	-	-
62	Endocast retaining the shape of the skull and small extremely fragile and damage bone fragments of frontal, R parietal and occipital portions **(Fig. 3.58 to 3.62)**; portion of L parietal and temporal are attached on it. Foramen magnum present, frontal bone extremely damage and part of orbital border present, R mastoid process partly present. Around 30 small to medium skull bone chips are present. Facial bones are extremely fragile and mainly cast is retaining the shape of the bone. Some traces of nasal bones, extremely damage part of L zygomatic bone present, maxilla extremely damage and mainly cast retaining the shape and also holding teeth and root in it. Part of palate present.	**Maxilla**: RPm2 (isolated, broken crown and part of root). Sample is taken for isotope analysis. LPm1 (isolated broken crown) broken for sample collection. LM1 (isolated fragment of tooth and root present), RM1 (*in situ*), RM2 (crown broken, root and part of dentine present *in situ*). Root of LPm1, LPm2 and LM1 present *in situ*. LM2 only the caste of root present with few traces. LM3 isolated, state of crown calcification uncertain and sample has been taken by Ben	-	-	-

Specimen No	Skull	Dentition	Thoracic Cage	Upper Extremity	Lower Extremity
64	-	-	One block of soil, broken into two pieces contains 6 left ribs, 5 thoracic vertebrae and two lumbar vertebrae. Another block of soil contains another three lumbar vertebrae and upper body of sacrum. Extremely damage and individual identification has been done on the basis of *in situ* preservation. Lower body of sacrum broken and missing.	**Humerus:** L distal half present. Both epicondyles and trochlea entirely preserved. Extremely damaged shaft. **Ulna:** L almost entire ulna present except distal end but damage shaft. **Radius:** L almost entire bone, except proximal end, persevered into one big and two small fragments. **Metacarpals:** L 1st entirely preserved with partly damage extremity. Preservation is moderate. 2nd proximal end preserved with partly damage proximity shaft.	**Pelvis:** L almost entire side present into two fragments, one of iliac crest attached to the sacrum, another unidentified, sciatic notch partly damage, Ilium, acetabulum, part of ischium and pubic present. **(Fig. 3.63) Femur:** R almost complete in 2 fragments, big fragment comprising head and entire shaft, without greater trochanter, medium and small fragments of distal end. Condyles are extremely damage and partly preserve; L almost complete in 2 pieces, proximal end broken from shaft and attached into acetabulum cavity of L pelvis bone. Preservation of shaft and distal end is better than the R side. A small portion of proximal shaft broken and missing. Anterior surface is better preserved than the posterior surface. **Patella:** R medial half, extremely damage attached to the distal potion of the right femur. **Tibia:** R proximal half extremely damage shaft; L almost entire bone present, distal extremity partly broken and missing. Preservation of proximal end and shaft is better than the right. **Fibula**: R extremely damage and fragile proximal end attached to R tibia; L extremely damage and fragile proximal end and shaft attached to the left tibia. One block of soil contains all the L sides **Tarsal, Metatarsal** and few **Phalange**.

Specimen No	Skull	Dentition	Thoracic Cage	Upper Extremity	Lower Extremity
65	Around 5 small to medium sized fragments of mandible present. Side and individual identification is not possible. Extremely poor preservation.	**Maxilla:** RPm1? (isolated and root partly broken) sample taken for isotope analysis. **Mandible:** LM1 (isolated part of crown and root broken), LM2 (Isolated only a part of root broken). Unidentified root fragment.	-	-	-
66	Endocast retaining the shape and holds the entire R side of the skull with frontal, parietal, occipital, mastoid process and zygomatic arch **(Fig. 3.64 to 3.68)**. Portion of L frontal and part of occipital also present, foramen magnum present. Moderate condition of preservation. Around 30 small to medium skull chips, Facial bones are extremely damage, R preserved better than the L side, R orbit with part of orbital border, zygomatic bone present, part of R maxillary cast present with dental root, nasal bones are extremely damage and only traces are present. Traces of L orbit, maxilla and zygomatic bones present.	Root of maxillary RI2, RPm2, RM1 and RM2 (with part of dentine) present *in situ*. Few dentine fragments of maxillary RM3 sample was taken for isotope analysis, and few unidentified root and crown fragments.	A small fragment of extremely fragile vertebral spine.	-	-
67	Almost complete skull with highly eroded surface, partly broken frontal, parietal and occipital, almost complete facial portion with partly broken orbital border and nasal bones **(Fig. 3. 67 to 3. 73)**. Maxilla extremely damage and broken into many parts, cast holds teeth in many places. Mandible attached with the skull, R vertical and horizontal ramus damaged with extremely	**Maxilla:** RI1 (extremely damage), LI1 (empty socket), RI2 (extremely damage and traces of enamel), LI2 (extremely damage traces of enamel), RC (empty socket), LC (extremely damage partly preserved dentine), RPm1-Pm2 (with traces of root), LPm1-Pm2 (with partly preserved dentine), RM1 (with traces of root), LM1 (with broken crown), RLM2, **Mandible:** LC, Only portion	One block of soil containing 8 thoracic vertebra, two lumber vertebra and 7 pair of ribs and both clavicles, another block of soil containing 3 lumbar vertebrae with 2 ribs, extremely damage and eroded **(Fig. 3.74)**.	**Humerus:** R block of soil which contains thoracic cage also has extremely damage shaft portion, both extremities missing; L isolated, extremely damage shaft, both extremities missing, one distal end of humerus without side identification. **Ulna:** L intact proximal end with partly damage olecranon process and two proximal shaft fragments extremely fragile.	**Pelvis:** Soil block containing three lumber vertebras also contains extremely damage sacrum body and RL iliac blades, L better preserved than R. **Femur:** R distal half shaft fragment, extremely damage, distal end missing; L almost entire femur preserved into one big and other medium fragment, both extremities missing, lesser trochantor partly preserved, relatively better preserved

Specimen No	Skull	Dentition	Thoracic Cage	Upper Extremity	Lower Extremity
	eroded surface, in many places only cast present, RL coronoid and condyels extremely damaged, L vertical and horizontal ramus are better preserved than R but damaged surface, L coronoid and condyels better preserved. Chin part missing.	of root is present in case of LPm1and Pm2. RLM1 (broken, extremely damage, small fragment), RM3 (intact present *in situ*), LM3 (isolated broken crown, sampled for isotope analysis).			than other parts of bone. **Tibia:** R almost complete with broken extremities, extremely damaged; L four small and medium fragments of shaft, both extremities are missing, extremely damaged. **Fibula:** R broken parts of shafts attached with R tibia, extremely damaged condition. L very small fragile portion of distal shaft. Around 20 small to medium soil blocks containing bone and long bone chips.

Figure 3.1: Burial 2, norma frontalis

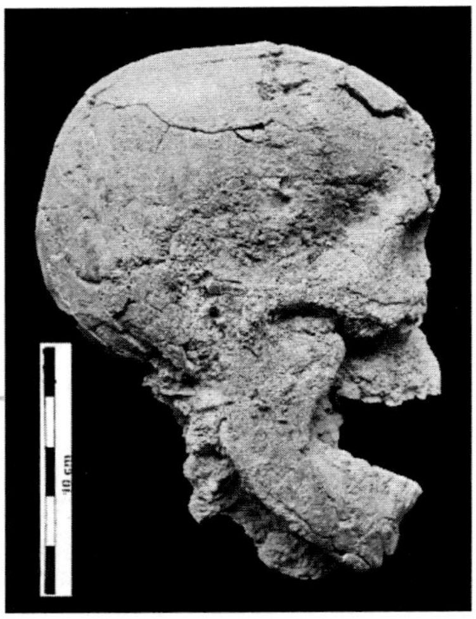

Figure 3.2: Burial 2, R norma lateralis

Figure 3.3: Burial 2, norma verticalis

Figure 3.4: Burial 2, norma occipitalis

Figure 3.5: Burial 3, norma verticalis

Figure 3.6: Burial 3, R norma lateralis

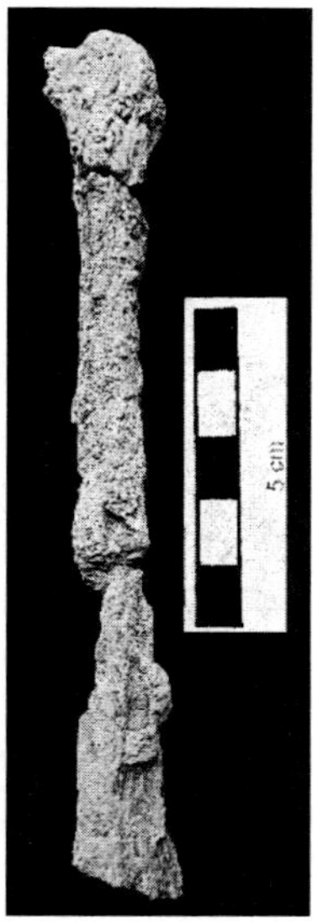

Figure 3.7: Burial 5, R humerus

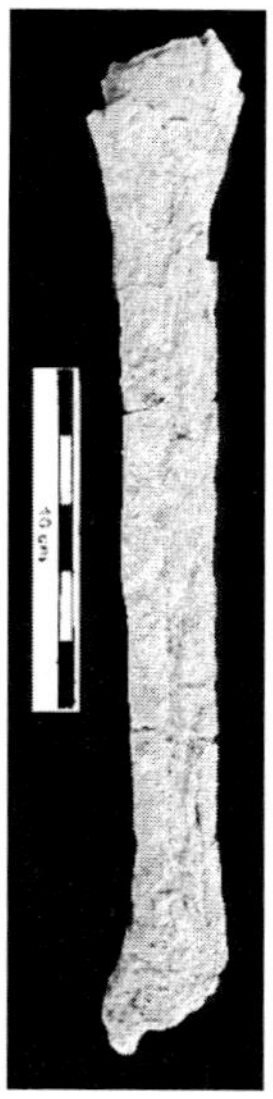

Figure 3.9: Burial 10, L tibia

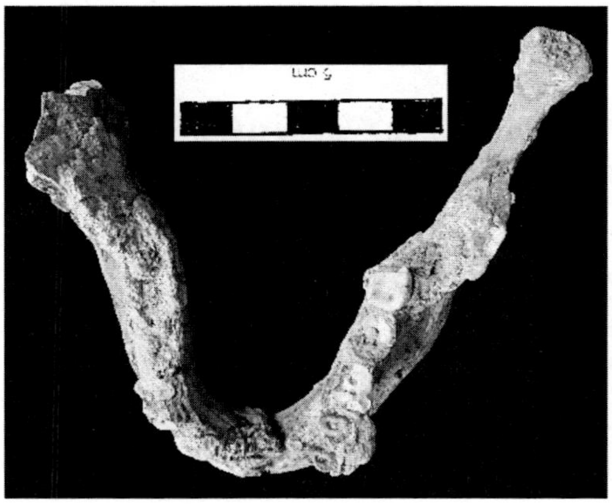

Figure 3.8: Burial 6, complete mandible

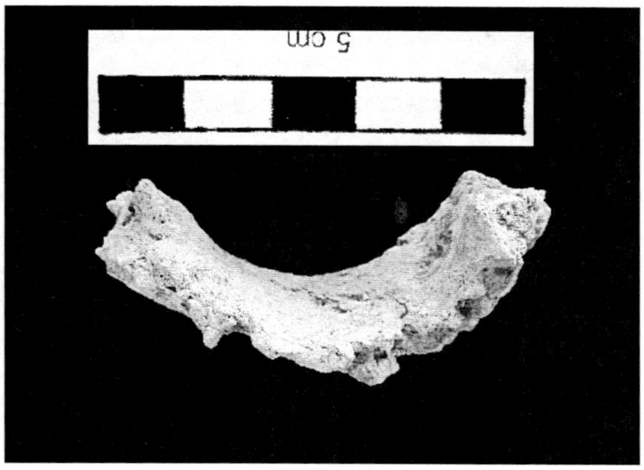

Figure 3.10: Burial 11, mandible

Figure 3.11: Burial 14, norma frontalis

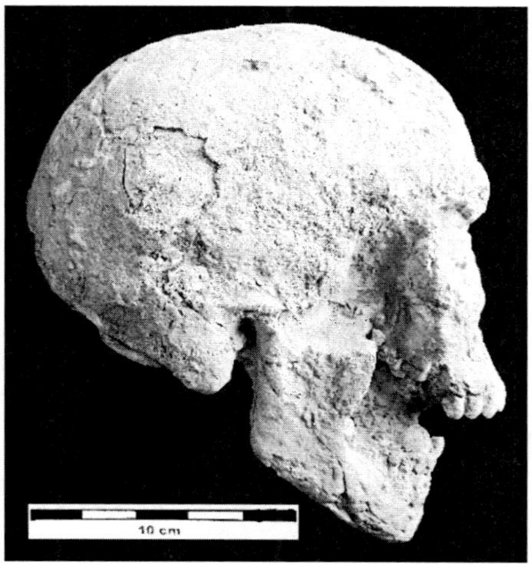

Figure 3.12: Burial 14, norma lateralis

Figure 3.13: Burial 14, norma verticalis

Figure 3.14: Burial 14, norma occipitalis

Figure 3.15: Burial 15, L norma lateralis

Figure 3.16: Burial 18, norma frontalis

Figure 3.17: Burial 18, noma verticalis

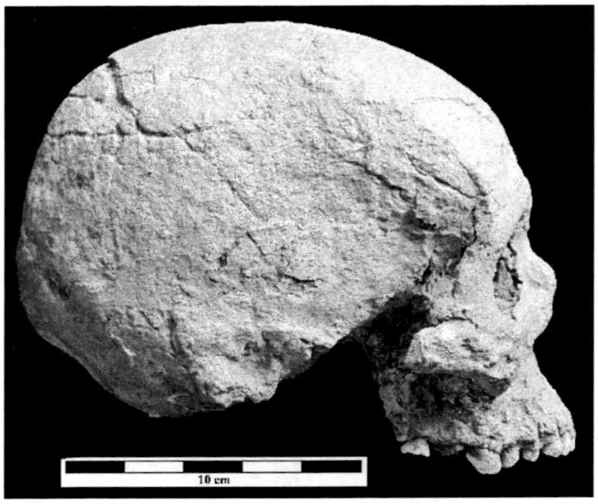

Figure 3.18: Burial 18, R norma lateralis

Figure 3.19: Burial 18, norma occipitalis

Figure 3.20: Burial 18, norma basalaris

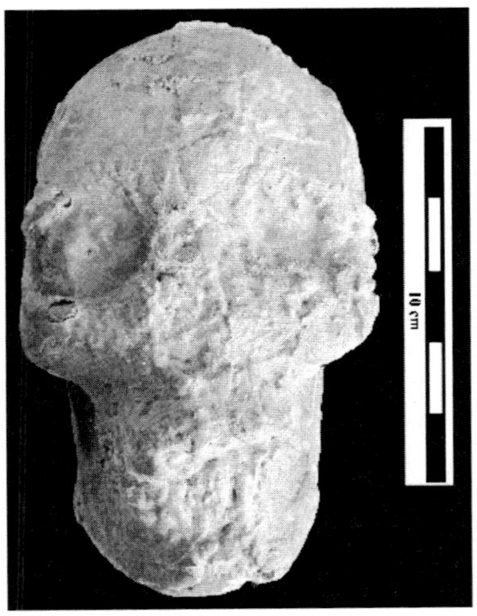

Figure 3.21: Burial 20, norma frontalis

Figure 3.22: Burial 20, norma vericalis

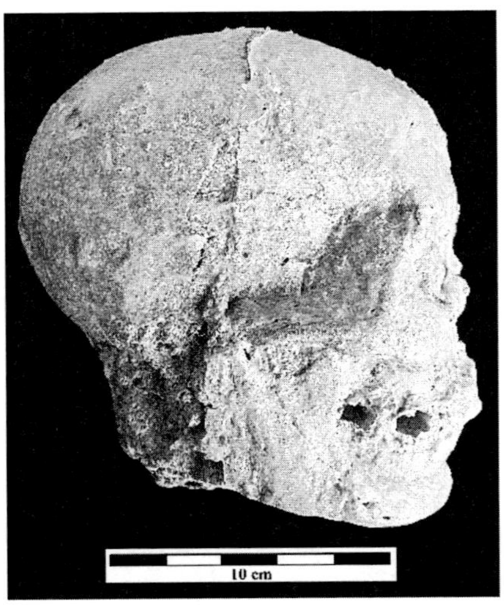

Figure 3.23: Burial 20, R norma lateralis

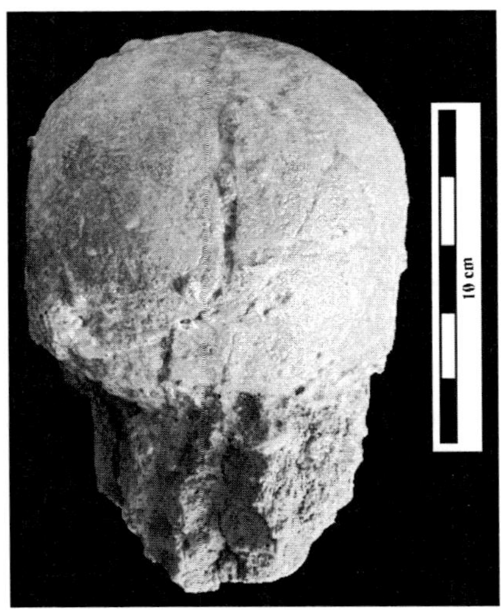

Figure 3.24: Burial 20, norma occipitalis

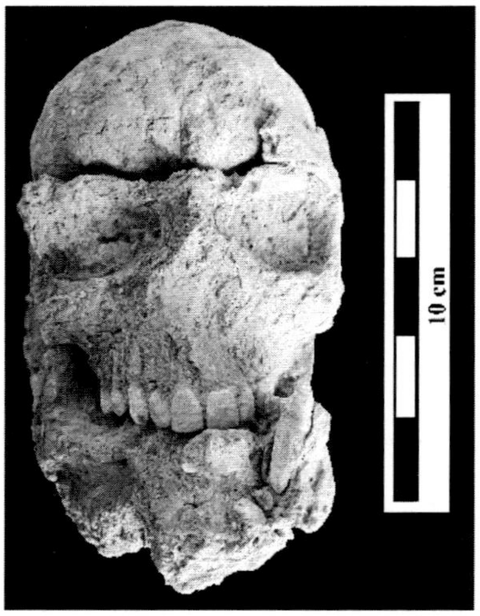

Figure 3.25: Burial 23, norma frontalis

Figure 3.26: Burial 23, norma verticalis

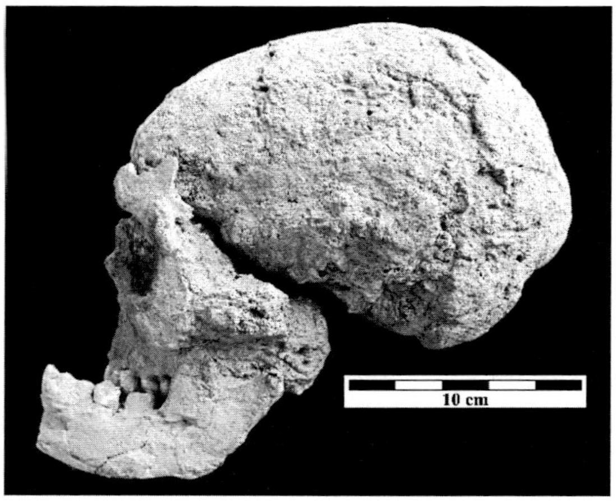

Figure 3.27: Burial 23, L norma lateralis

Figure 3.28: Burial 23, norma occipitalis

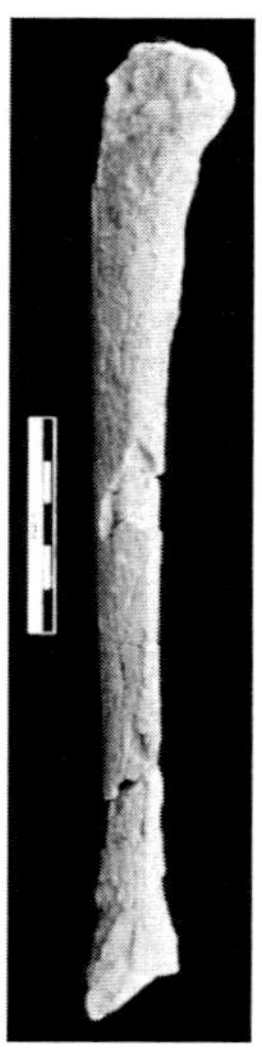
Figure 3.29: Burial 25, R tibia

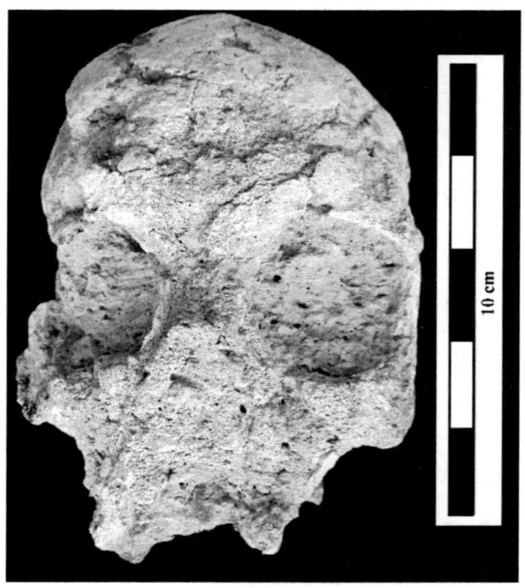

Figure 3.30: Burial 26, norma frontalis

Figure 3.31: Burial 26, norma verticalis

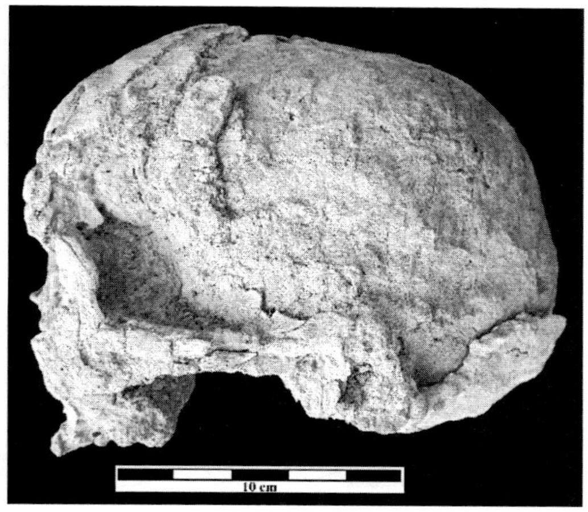

Figure 3.32: Burial 26, L norma lateralis

Figure 3.33: Burial 26, norma occipitalis

Figure 3.34: Burial 26, norma basalaris

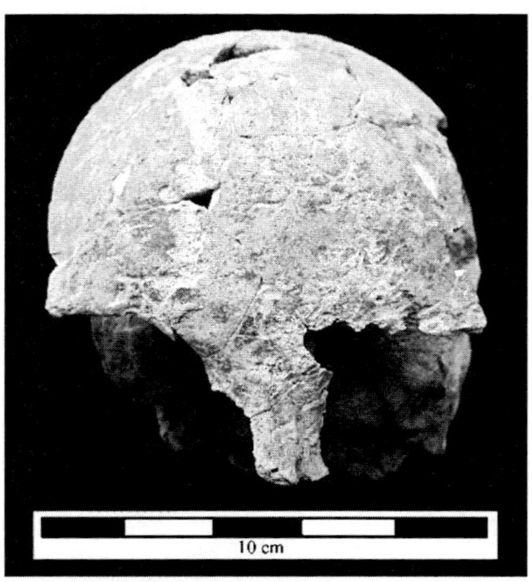

Figure 3.35: Burial 32, norma frontalis

Figure 3.36: Burial 32, norma verticalis

Figure 3.37: Burial 32, R norma lateralis

Figure 3.38: Burial 32, norma occipitalis

Figure 3.39: Burial 32, thoracic region in soil block

Figure 3.40: Burial 34, norma verticalis

Figure 3.41: Burial 34, L norma lateralis

Figure 3.42: Burial 34, norma occipitalis

Figure 3.43: Burial 39a, L norma lateralis

Figure 3.44: Burial 39b, norma verticalis

Figure 3.45: Burial 39b, norma occipitalis

Figure 3.46: Burial 39b, norma basalaris

Figure 3.47: Burial 45, norma frontalis

Figure 3.48: Burial 45, norma verticalis

Figure 3.49: Burial 45, R norma lateralis

Figure 3.50: Burial 45, norma occipitalis

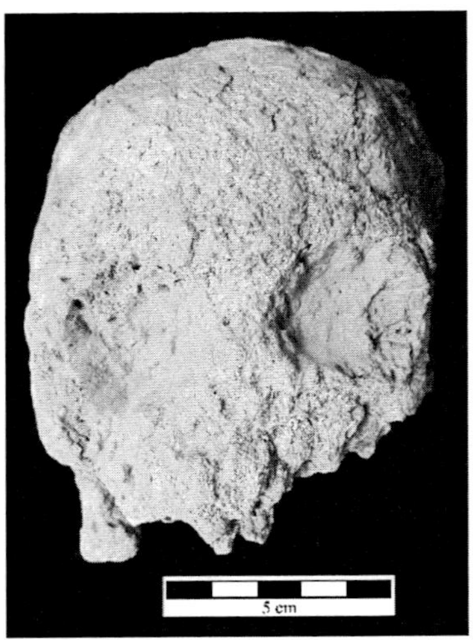

Figure 3.51: Burial 52, norma frontalis

Figure 3.52: Burial 52, norma verticalis

Figure 3.53: Burial 52, R norma lateralis

Figure 3.54: Burial 53, norma frontalis

Figure 3.55: Burial 53, R norma lateralis

Figure 3.56: Burial 53, norma occipitalis

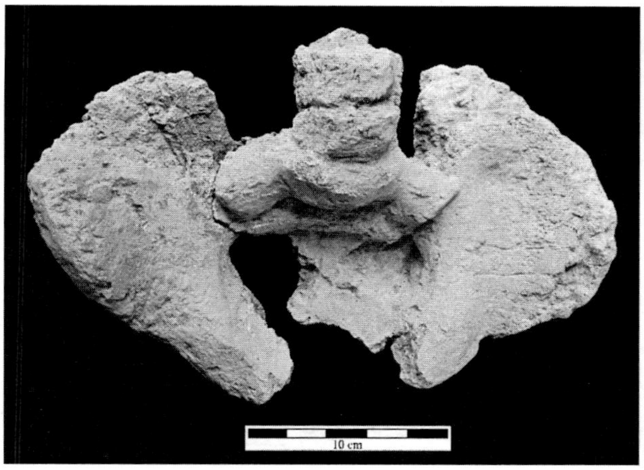

Figure 3.57: Burial 53, pelvis

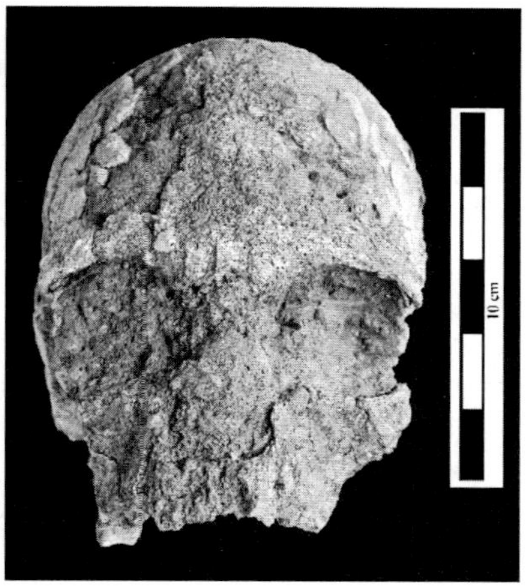

Figure 3.58: Burial 62, norma frontalis

Figure 3.59: Burial 62, norma verticalis

Figure 3.60: Burial 62, L norma lateralis

Figure 3.61: Burial 62, norma occipitalis

Figure 3.62: Burial 62, norma basalaris

Figure 3.63: Burial 64, lumber and L pelvic bone

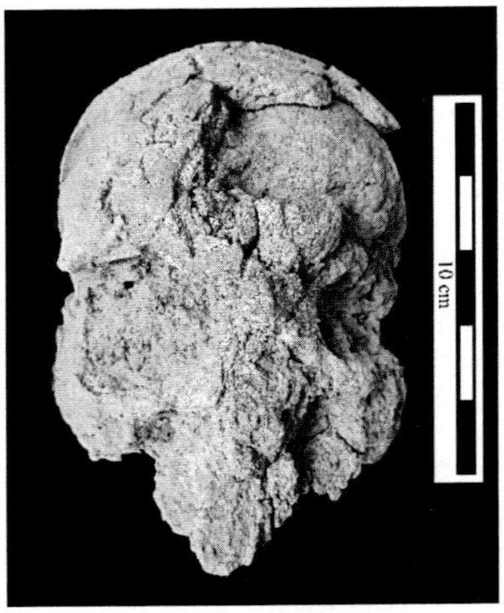

Figure 3.64: Burial 66, norma forntalis

Figure 3.65: Burial 66, norma verticalis

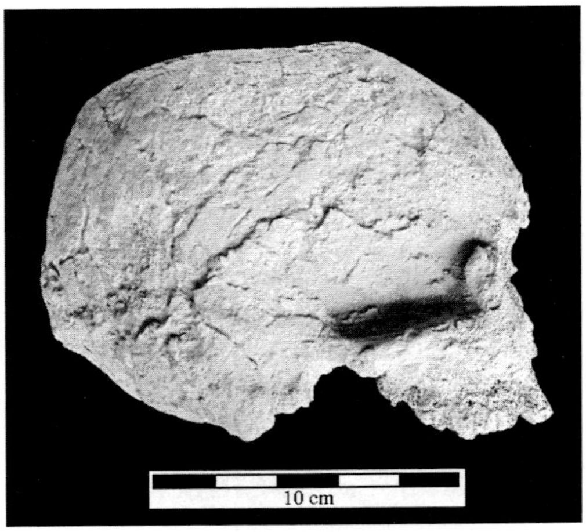

Figure 3.66: Burial 66, R norma lateralis

Figure 3.67: Burial 66, norma occipitalis

Figure 3.68: Burial 66, norma basalaris

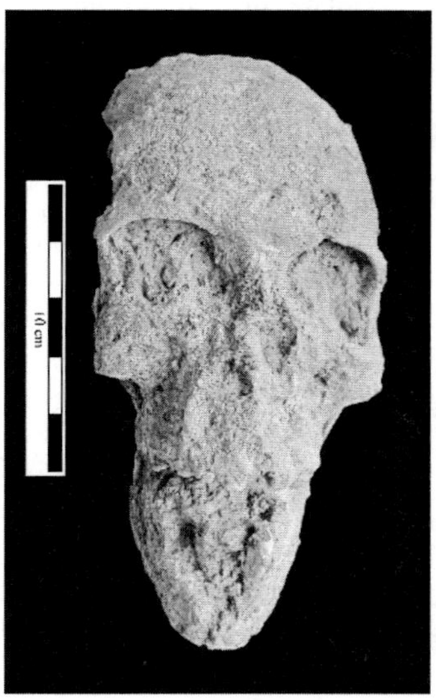

Figure 3.69: Burial 67, norma frontalis

Figure 3.70: Burial 67, norma verticalis

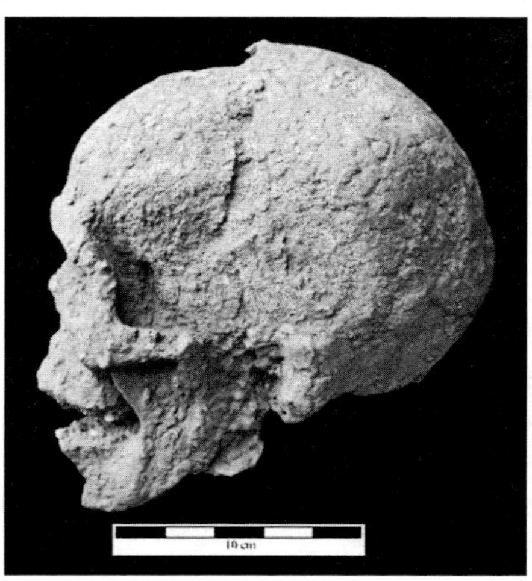

Figure 3.71: Burial 67, L norma lateralis

Figure 3.72: Burial 67, R norma lateralis

Figure 3.73: Burial 67, norma occipitalis

Figure 3.74: Burial 67, thoracic region in soil block

4

Demographic Profile of Farmana Skeletal Assemblage

While doing the age and sex identification several limitations were encountered. The main hurdle was the preservation. Many individuals are represented by skull molded in soil or endocast. The age estimation is based on the dental attrition and for some individuals, it is based on the stages of suture closure at various points which are recommended by Buikstra and Ubelaker (1994). For young individuals, the length of long bones become the criteria for age estimation as no other criteria were available for observations. In certain cases, it was also difficult to ascertain age brackets. In those cases, age was based on some morphological characters and categorized as sub-adult or adult.

Several individuals were missing bone parts having specific morphological features indicative of their sex. Most of the skeletons are devoid of preserved pelvis bone which made sex identification very difficult. Many times sex identification is based on morphological appearance (robust or gracile) of bone. This is not a reliable criterion and is mentioned while discussing it individual-wise.

The skeletal assemblage was categories subsequent age categorization:

Infant: 0 – 1 year
Early Child: 1 – 5 years of age
Late Child: 6 – 11 years
Adolescent: 12 – 16 years
Young adult: 16 – 31 years
Middle-aged adult: 31- 45
Old age adult: 45 +

Burial 1

Age estimation: Greater trochanter of this individual is fused with the shaft, which generally fuses in between 16-18 years for male and 14-16 years for females. The proximal epiphysis of the tibia is completely fused with the shaft which fuses between 15-19 years in males and from 13-19 years in the female. The molar which is identified as 3rd right molar do not have attrition on the occlusal level. On the basis of tooth eruption and epiphyseal fusion of bones, the individual is identified as a young adult ranging from 18-20 years.

Sex determination: Robust nature of long bones and extremely developed lesser trochanter of the femur and heavy muscular attachment help to identify the sex of the individual as male. (Fig. 4.1)

Burial 2

Age estimation: The cranial suture exhibit almost complete closure at the lambdoidal point and the average dental attrition is in grades of 6 to 9, which indicates the age of the individual around 50 years. (Fig. 4.2)

Figure 4.1: Burial 1, strongly developed lesser tronchanter on R femur

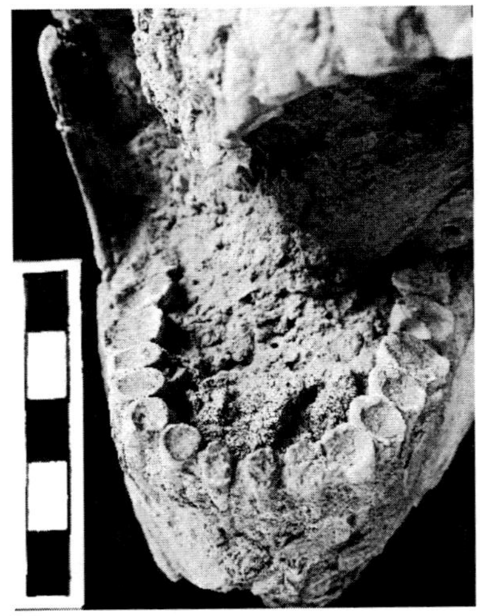

Figure 4.2: Burial 2, wear pattern on mandibular dentition

Sex determination: The sex of this individual is based on the morphology of skull. the Nuchal Crest: Grade 1; Mastoid Process: Grade 4; Supra-Orbital Ridge: Grade 1; Mental eminence: Grade: 2; The grades giving more female-like appearance to the individual, whereas muscularity present in the mastoid and in the gonial angle indicating the sex of the individual as male. To summarise this individual is appearing more of female than male.

Burial 3

Age estimation: From the nature of long bones and crania, it can be assumed that this individual is of late adolescent or in the stage of an early adult. Determination of exact age is not possible due to poor preservation.

Burial 5

Age estimation: The age estimation for this individual is based on the general appearance of bones and maxillary second deciduous molar (Rdm2) which shows eruption. Based on these criteria the individual was around 3.5-4 years.

Burial 6

Age estimation: This is partially represented individual. Alveolar resorption and grade 5 dental attrition put the age of the individual as around 40-45 years (Fig. 4.3). (see next page)

Sex determination: It is only based on the mandible which is almost complete. The gonial angle of the mandible is 123°, and mental eminence score is of grade 1. Gracile nature of the humerus indicates the female sex of the individual. This should be read with caution.

Burial 8

Age estimation: Distal end of the femur and the proximal end of tibia indicates complete fusion of diaphysis to epiphysis indicating adult status of the individual. Though proper age bracket cannot be determined.

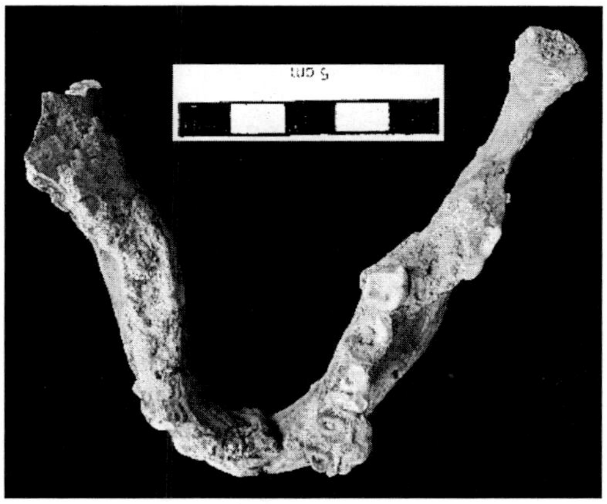

Figure 4.3: Burial 6, mandible

Sex determination: Even though the border of the sciatic notch is broken from one side, the alignment of the notch indicating more male-like appearance grading around 3. As well as prominently developed linea-aspera help to tentatively identify the sex of the individual as male. Although this should be read with caution.

Burial 10

Age estimation: Distal end of the humerus indicates complete fusion of diaphysis to epiphysis specifying the adult status of the individual. Exact age cannot be estimated.

Sex determination: The individual is probably a male, based on moderate bone structure. Though it is difficult to confirm it.

Burial 11

Age estimation: The only part of mandible preserved for analysis. On the basis of dental attrition grades, the age was probably around 45±5 years old.

Sex determination: The sex determination has been conducted on the field while observing the specimen *insitu*. Female sex is identified after observing the pubis angle. As the bones were extremely fragile they were not sent to a lab for further analysis.

Burial 14

Age estimation: The individual is adult. Grades of dental attrition show that the individual was around 20-25 years old, the third molar was erupted and was in the occlusal level and shows a minimum level of attrition of grade 1. The completely fused right humerus shaft indicates the age of the individual is around 25 years. (Fig. 4.4)

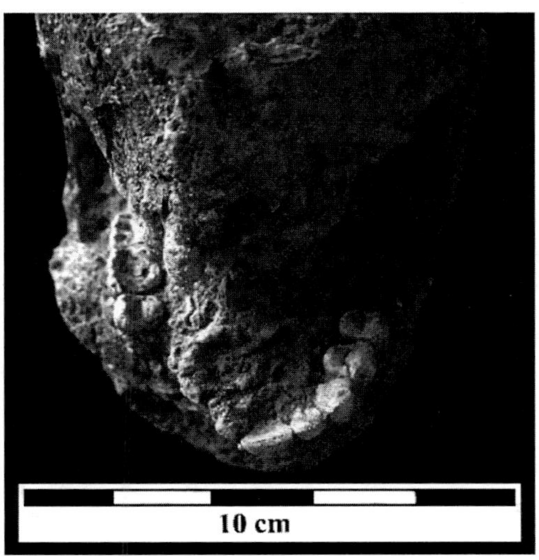

Figure 4.4: Burial 14, mandible

Sex determination: Sex identification is based on skull morphology including Mastoid process: 4; Supra orbital ridge: 4; Mental eminence: 4; Nuchal crest: 2; Gonial angle: 123° degree.

The individual is robust. Gradation of the mastoid process, supra orbital ridge, and mental eminence suggest this individual is male, whereas the nuchal crest grade and gonial angle suggest a female like a feature. From the general robusticity, heavy muscular attachment and from the grade observation, the sex of the individual can be concluded as male.

Burial 15

Age estimation: Both the maxillary M1s are in the process of crown calcification and was inside the crypt. The formation of M1 crown calcification completes at the age of 2.5-3 years old.

In this case, around 2/3rd of the crown formation has completed. This indicates that the age of the child was around 2 years old.

Burial 18

Age estimation: Only skull of this individual is present. The grades of dental attrition are in between grade 5 to 7. The cranial sutures also show almost advance stages of closure. This indicates the age of the individual as 40-45 years. (Fig. 4.5)

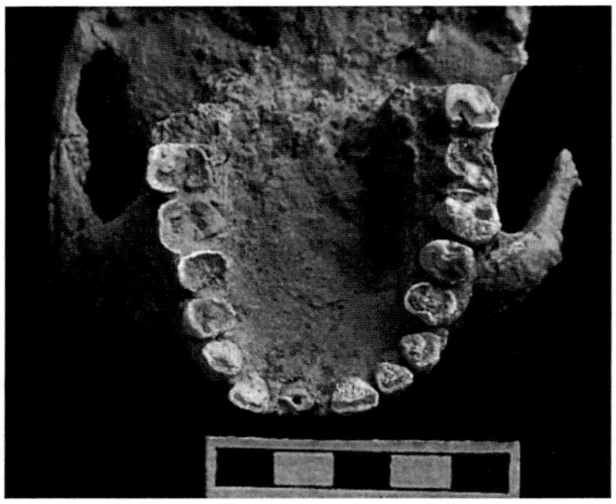

Figure 4.5: Burial 18, maxilla

Sex determination: The sex of this skeleton is based on skull morphology. The grades of the nuchal crest- 1; mastoid process- 2; supra orbital margin- 2; supra orbital ridge- 3; gonial angle- 125° degree (Fig. 4.6). Except for the development of supra orbital ridge, the other features suggest this individual as female.

Burial 20

Age estimation: Age of this individual based on the status of suture closure which is in advance stage. The dental attrition is of grade 7 and 4 on the maxillary right 1st and 3rd molar respectively. This indicates the age of the individual is around 35-40 years.

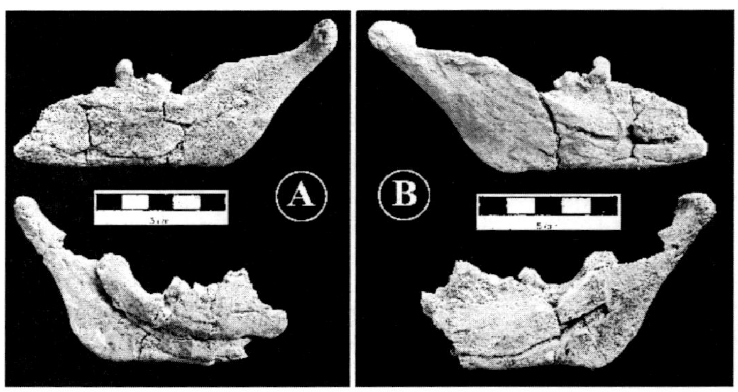

Figure 4.6: Burial 18, mandible

Sex determination: The grades of skull morphology including nuchal crest grade 2, mastoid process grade 3, supra orbital line 2, mental eminence 2 is more of a female in character. The individual is a female though bones are quite thick and broad.

Burial 23

Age estimation: Mandibular 3rd right molar is present and indicates that it erupts, which happens at the age of 18 to 25 and 2nd right molar which is present, erupts at the age of 12-13. Crowns of right 1st and 2nd molar are intact and without much of attrition. This indicates the age of the individual around 18 - 25 years old (Fig. 4.7).

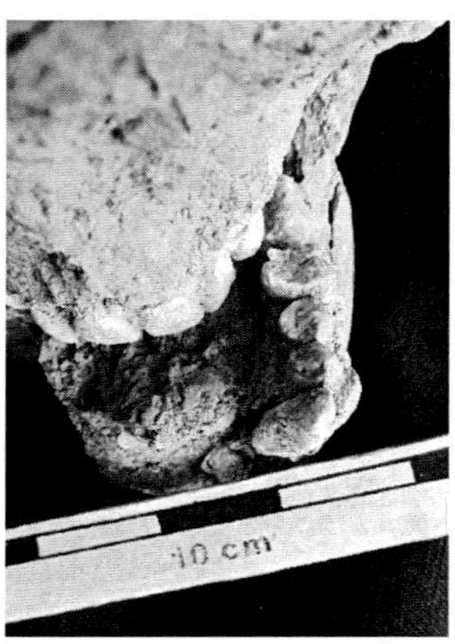

Figure 4.7: Burial 23, mandible

Sex determination: The skull is extremely damaged and sex determination is only based on the supra orbital margin (grade 1). Although this is not confirmative but it points towards female sex of the individual. This identification should be considered with some limitations.

Burial 25

Age estimation: This individual is an Adult individual on the basis of bone size and morphology.

Sex determination: Though the skull and pelvis are absent, sex of the individual is identified as male on the basis of the robusticity related to heavy muscular attachment. But this should be read with caution.

Burial 26

Age estimation: The attrition pattern of maxillary Pm2 and RLM2 indicate the age of the individual as around 40-45 years old. (Fig. 4.8).

Figure 4.8: Burial 26, maxillary Pm2

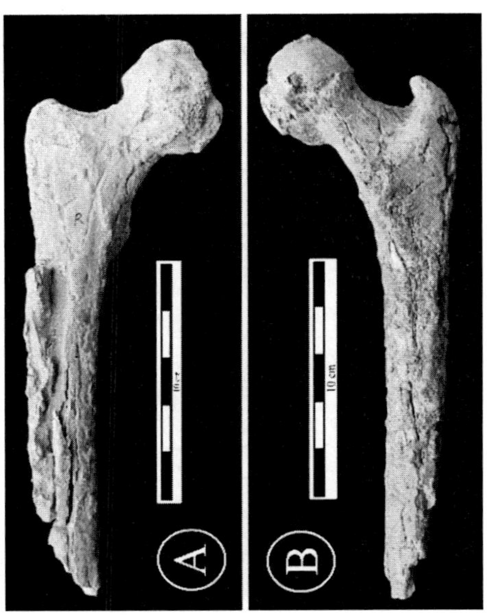

Figure 4.9: Burial 32, a. anterior of left femur, b. posterior side

Sex determination: The identification of female sex for this individual is based only on the Supra orbital margin (grade 1) morphology.

Burial 28

Age estimation: In the laboratory only the endocast is present but in the burial pit long bones were present and *insitu* measurement of the femur was taken in the field. The femoral shaft is 16 cm which was compared with the reference skeleton present in the laboratory. On that basis, the individual is identified as around 2.5 to 3 years old, but the exact age estimation was not possible.

Burial 32

Age estimation: On the basis of cranial suture closure (grade-A), delicate nature of the skull bones and slender long bones put the age of this individual young adult of about 18±1 years old. (Fig. 4.9)

Sex determination: For sexing this individual the morphological features of the skull are used. The grades of supra orbital margin (grade 1), supra orbital ridge (grade 2), mastoid process (grades 3?) and nuchal crest (grade 2) shows delicate morphology. Though the mastoid process is quite developed, the other grades and the gracile and slender nature of the long bones help to identify the sex of the individual as female.

Burial 34

Age estimation: Only cranial cap is represented for this specimen. This is probably of an adult individual on the basis of the size of crania.

Sex determination: The cranial morphology including nuchal crest is of grade 2 and mastoid process of grade 4. The mastoid process showing a greater development and putting the sex of the individual in the male category but the thin nature of bone and the nuchal crest of grade 2 indicating it as female which should be considered with caution.

Burial 39A

Age estimation: On the basis of lambdoid and sagittal suture closure, which is of grade 2 where the suture closure is significant but not complete, the age of the individual is presumed to be around 45 years.

Sex determination: On the basis of the nuchal crest grade 1, the sex of the individual is predicate as a female.

Burial 39B

Age estimation: On the basis of suture closure grade 2 for the coronal and sagittal and grade 1 for lambdoidal, as well as traces of attrition on a molar (grade identification not possible), the age assigned to the individual is around 45-50 years old.

Sex determination: On the basis of nuchal crest grade 4, thick nature of skull bone and robust condition of the mandible, the sex of the individual is identified as probable male.

Burial 41

Age estimation: All maxillary teeth have broken roots which hamper the understanding of root calcification status. Both maxillary M2s are isolated and were inside the crypt. They show complete crown calcification and no evidence of the beginning of root calcification. Generally, crown calcification of M2 completes around 7-8 years and an eruption occurs at the age of 10-12 years. I2 which was also in the crypt but shows complete crown calcification was in the process of eruption. Crown calcification completes at the age of 5-6 years and eruption occurs at the age of 7-8 years for I2. This gives the minimum age of the individual as around 6 years and maximum as around 8 years. Canine also shows a complete crown calcification and it is also inside the crypt. Crown calcification of canine gets over at the age of 6-7 years. To sum up the age of the child is around 7-8 years.

Burial 45

Age estimation: This individual is sub-adult, all the permanent dentition other than M3 are erupted and are in the occlusal level. The second molar erupts at the age of 12-13, the premolar and second molar shows a minimum attrition grade. The first molars of both the sides show an attrition grade of 4 and 5. The cranial cap is very thin indicating a young age. The size of the mandible is also very small in comparison with adult mandibles. On the basis of all these observations, the age of the individual is above 13 years and other attrition grades suggesting not more than 15 years. To sum up the age bracket of this individual is 13-15 years old.

Burial 47

Age estimation: Maxillary LM2 was inside the crypt and showing almost complete crown formation, this indicates the age of the individual as around 7-8 years old. Maxillary RPm1, LPm2, and RC show complete crown calcification. Roots are broken but indicate the beginning of root calcification, though the extent is not known. This also indicates a similar age group of 7-8 years. Mandibular LI2 shows a complete crown calcification. I2 erupts at the age of 8-9 years and root calcification completes at the age of 10-11 years. In this case, incisor root is broken but indicates the beginning of root calcification. The age of the child was around 7-8 years. Small skull size and very thin nature of bones also indicate a young age of the individual.

Burial 48

Age estimation: There are no cranial and dental elements present for this individual therefore the exact estimation of age is not possible. The fused long bones help to identify the age of the individual as an adult and probably around 20±5 years.

Sex determination: Robust nature of long bone and extremely developed linea aspera of femur indicate the probable male sex for this individual.

Burial 50A

Age estimation: The cranial bones are quite thick and developed. Developed mastoid process indicates an adult age for this individual probably a young adult. Partially preserved open lambdoidal suture also indicate the young age of this individual.

Sex determination: Sex determination of this individual is been done on the basis of the nuchal crest and mastoid process. Nuchal crest showing a grade of 2 and the mastoid process is showing a grade of 4 (Fig. 4.10), this indicates the male sex of this individual. The sex determination of this individual should be read with caution as there are no other indicators available for inspection.

Figure 4.10: Burial 50a, left mastoid

Burial 50B

Age estimation: There are no cranial and dental elements for this specimen. On the basis of field photographs where the skull is present and long bones, it has been concluded that this individual was an adult though exact age cannot be assigned. The observations were made on the field indicate an age of 30-35 years for this individual.

Sex determination: On the basis of sciatic notch grade 2 (?) and robust nature of bones and field report, it has been concluded that this individual is a robust female (Fig. 4.11).

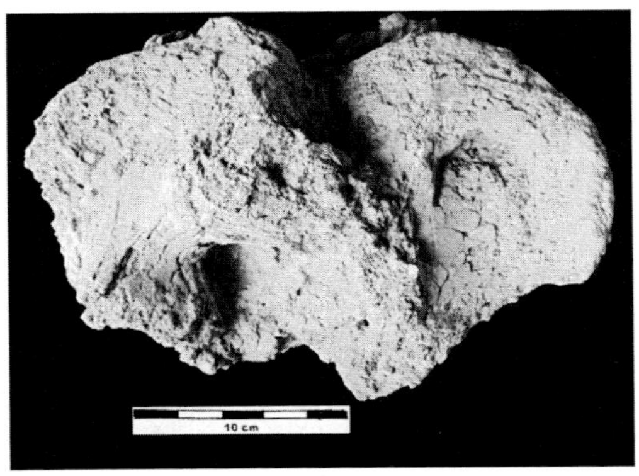

Figure 4.11: Burial 50b, right and left Pelvic bones

Burial 52

Age estimation: Maxillary Rdm2 is on the occlusal level. It erupts at the age of 32 months. Maxillary I1 which erupts at the age of 9-12 months, showing an attrition of grade 4. Permanent I2 is inside the crypt with almost complete crown calcification. The crown calcification of I2 completes at the age of 4-5 years. These help to identify the age of the individual as around 3.5 years old.

Burial 53

Age estimation: The status of sagittal suture is of grade 1 indicating minimum to moderate percentage of closure has occurred. Tentatively age of this individual is around 30 years.

Sex determination: Only extremely damage skull and pelvic is present. Supra orbital ridge shows grade 1, nuchal crest show grade 1, the sciatic notch is more of wide and shallow. These criteria help to identify the sex of the individual as a female.

Burial 54

Age estimation: The nature of bones and the presence of mandibular RM1 with calcified root help to identify the age of the individual as an adult. The tentative age was identified as around 30 years.

Sex determination: This individual was not completely present for the analysis due to fragile nature. The observations were made on the field and the morphology of the pelvis *insitu* suggested male sex for this specimen.

Burial 58

Age estimation: The only mandibular RM2 is available, which erupts at the age of 12-13. It shows wear pattern of grade 2. This indicates the age of the individual was probably around 20 years or belonging to a young adult category.

Burial 62

Age estimation: On the basis of thin nature of the skull bone, the fresh condition of molar, as well as pre molar with a minimal grade of attrition and in crypt condition of 3rd molar, the age of the individual, is assigned as around 15 years old or a late adolescent.

Sex determination: Preservation of skull is extremely bad, glabella, supra orbital margin, supra orbital ridge, the right mastoid process is extremely damaged. There is a bulging on the occipital lobe of the skull.

The exact grade identification is not possible, but they all are showing minimal development. This individual is probably female.

Burial 64

Age estimation: Cranial and dental elements are not present. Therefore, exact estimation of age is not possible, but the entirely fused long bones put the age of the individual as of adult and probably around 20 years. (Fig. 4.12) (see next page)

Sex determination: From the sciatic notch, robust nature of bone, linea aspera of the femur and developed mussel attachment, it is concluded that specimen was a male individual.

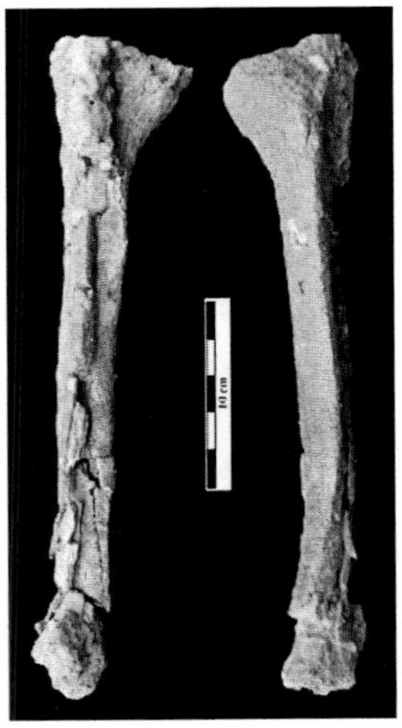

Figure 4.12: Burial 64, right and left tibiae

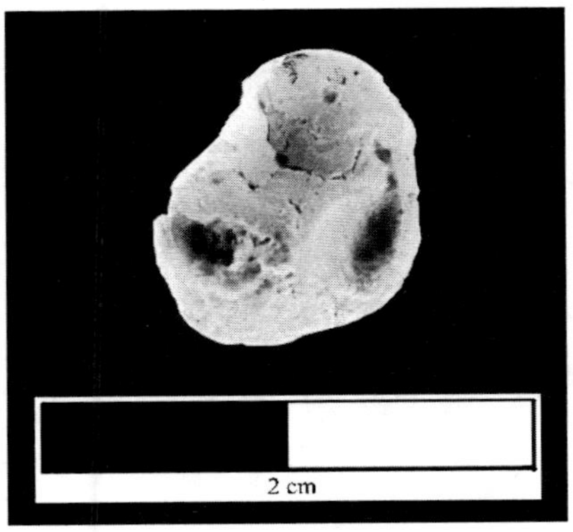

Figure 4.13: Burial 65, mandibular left first molar

Burial 65

Age estimation: Completely calcified crown and the root of mandibular left M1 and M2 indicate the age of the individual as an adult. The attrition grades on these teeth put the age of the individual as around 30 or middle-aged person or around 30 ± 5 years. (Fig. 4.13)

Burial 66

Age estimation: Thick skull bones and suture closure grade 2 of coronal and lambdoidal suture indicates the age of the individual as around 50 years. The exact age estimation is not possible.

Sex determination: Extremely damaged skull gives some morphological observations. Nuchal crest is of grade 5, mastoid process grade 5 with developed glabella region (grade estimation not possible due to damage condition) identify the male sex of the individual.

Burial 67

Age estimation: The attrition on the right mandibular molar and canine put the age of this individual around 35 years.

Sex determination: It is difficult to identify the sex of this individual. Cranial morphology including Nuchal Crest: 2 (?); Mastoid Process: 5; Supra orbital margin: 3; Supra orbital Ridge: 5 is observed. Even gonial angle is around 120 degree. Except for nuchal crest grade-2 (which is doubtful), other grades indicate male sex for this individual.

Sex identification is of individuals 58 and 65 not possible due to fragmentary nature of remains. One late adolescent is identified as female (specimen 62) which is included while discussing male-female categories. For three males and one female individual, age is only determined as an adult as exact age is not possible to estimate.

Table 4.1: The summery of age and sex categories from the Farmana

Age	Males (individual nos.)	Females (individual nos.)
Adolescent	-	62
Young	1, 14, 48, 50a, 54, 64	23, 32, 53
Middle aged	67	6, 26, 50b
Old aged	39b, 66	2, 11, 18, 20, 39a
Adult	8,10,25	34
Total	12	13

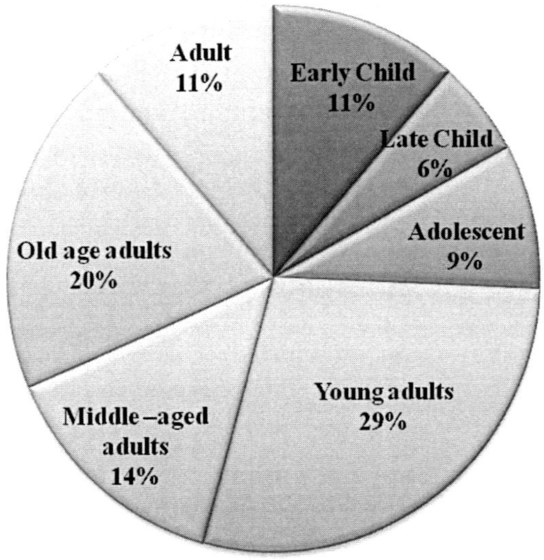

Figure 4.14: Graph showing age-wise percentage of Farmana skeletal assemblage

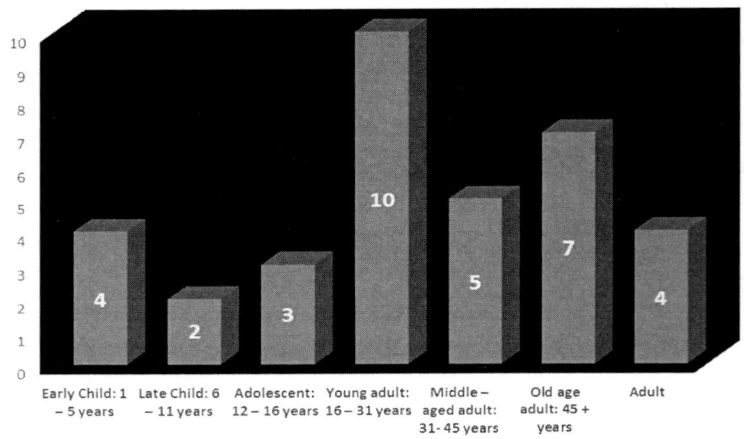

Figure 4.15: Graph showing the demographic profile of Farmana skeletal assemblage

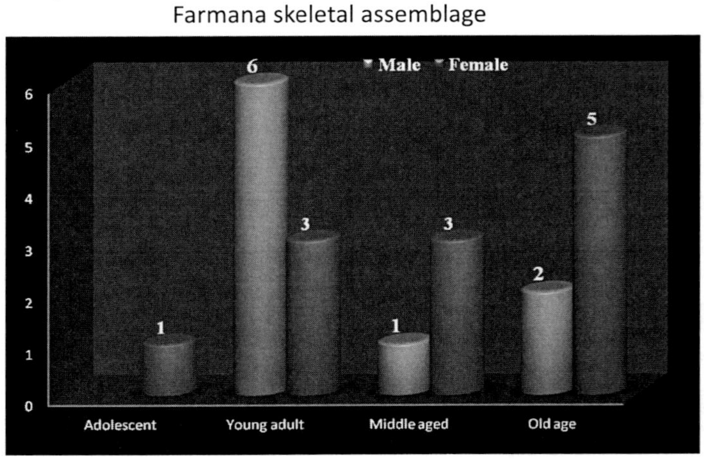

Figure 4.16: Graph showing age and sex wise distributions of Farmana skeletal remains

Farmana specimens are divided mainly into children (2 to 12 years), adolescent (13 -17 years) and adult (18 years onwards). Out of 35 specimens, there are 26 adults (Male – 12, Female – 12, Unidentified sex - 2), 5 adolescents (Early and Late) and 4 children (Graph 1). The youngest individual is around 2 year (skeleton No. 15) (Fig. 4.14 and 4.15). At the same time, it is interesting to note the age wise distribution of the skeletal series, where a maximum number of individuals is coming from young adult (18-25 y) category (graph. 2), which is followed by the 30s and 40s. It is also interesting to see that the young males are six in number in comparison with young females (3 individuals). The opposite trend is seen on the older individuals where females are more represented 3 in the middle-aged category and 5 individuals in old age than 1 male in middle-aged and 2 in old age individuals (Fig. 4.16).

5

Metric Analysis of Farmana Skeletal Remains

Taking measurements is very common practice in bio-archaeological analysis. From Harappan context, the cranial measurements played a very important role to assign particular skeletal population to a specific race in the early 70s and 80s. Cranial measurements are useful for calculating a cranial index which helps to understand the general shape and size of the skull.

There are numerous problems in taking these measurements which includes intra-observer and inter-observer errors. Although many cranial measurement manuals (Martin and Saller 1957, Sigh and Basin 1968, Brothwell 1981, Buikstra and Ubelakar 1994 etc.) describe the points from where measurements are to be taken, still it is difficult to avoid human errors.

Craniometric and osteometric methods used in this report follow Martin and Saller (1957) and cranial indices were calculated using Singh and Basin (1968). All the measurements, unless otherwise specified, are in millimetres. Cases where the reading is an estimated guess, the measurement is recorded in the bracket.

Table 5.1: Sites mentioned in the craniometric section with culture and chronology

Site	Culture	Chronology
Nevasa	Chalcolithic	2000 – 600 BCE
Kaothe	Chalcolithic	2000 – 1800 BCE
Inamgaon	Chalcolithic	2000 – 700 BCE
Harappa R-37	Harappa	2550-2030 BCE
Harappa Area G	Harappa	2000-1800 BCE
Harappa H-I	Harappa	2000 -1500 BCE
Harappa H-II	Harappa	2000 -1500 BCE
Mohenjodaro	Harappa	2600 – 1900 BCE
Burzahom	Neolithic	3000 – 1000 BCE
Piklihal	Neolithic	2000- 1250 BCE
Langhnaj	Mesolithic	2440-2160 BCE
Tekkalakota	Neolithic	2000 – 1800 BCE

There are around 18 skulls preserved, some are in bad and some are in moderate condition. Out of them, 14 crania was available for metric analysis. Within those 15 skulls, eight skulls provided a maximum number of measurements (Table 5.2a and b, Table 5.3a and b). They are 2, 14, 62, 66 and 67 (male individuals) and 18, 20 and 26 (female individuals). For rest seven crania, very few measurements are available. Out of seven, two crania 45 and 52, belongs to sub-adult individuals, aged 13-15 years and 3.5 years respectively. Measurements of these two specimens are not considered for any comparison because of its young age.

The cranial capacity was calculated only for two individuals (18 and 26). The cranial capacity of 45 years old female is 1256.80cc and 1280.97cc for around 45 years old female. Unfortunately, cranial capacity for a male could not be calculated due to bad preservation. Calculated indices are mentioned with cranial measurements but elaborately discussed in the morphology segment.

After the craniometric measurements, Farmana crania were compared with other sites belonging to different chronological and geographical brackets. The values are taken from the data published in Daimabad report (Walimbe 1986) and Nevasa (Mushrif and Walimbe 2006).

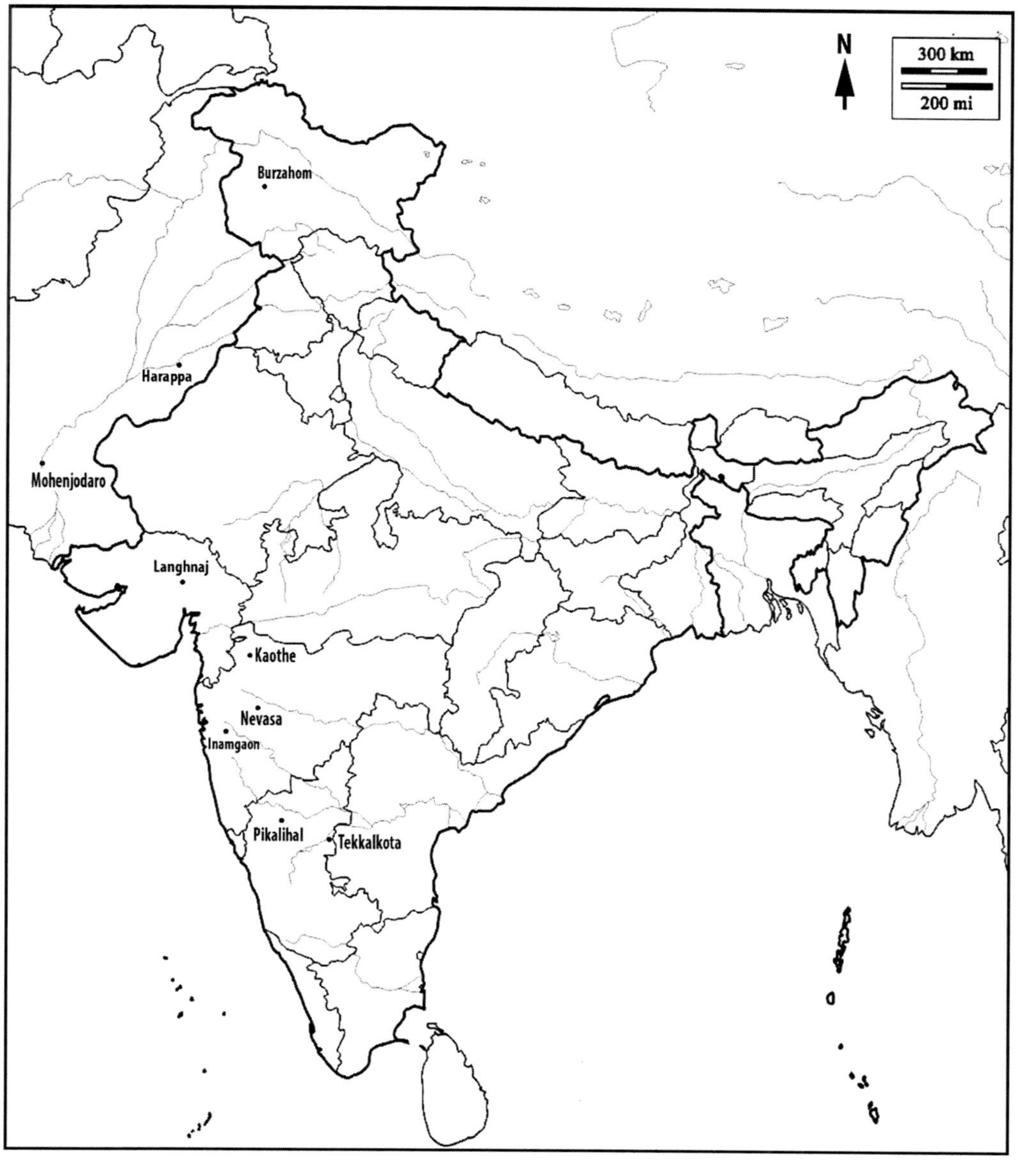

Fig.5.1: Approximate location of sites used for craniometric comparison

Table 5.2a: Craniometric observations on Farmana individuals from 2 to 34

Specimen number	02	14	18	20	23	26	32	34
Age	50+ y	20- 25 y	40-45 y	35-40 y	18-20 y	40-45 y	18-19 y	Adult
Sex	F	M	F	F	F	F	F	F?
Maximum cranial length (1)	177	(183)	184	177	-	179	179	-
Glabella inion length (2)	171	(180)	174	162	-	161	161	-
Glabella lambda length (3)	172	(181)	178	173	-	174	174	-
Maximum cranial breadth (8)	124	125	123	132	124	(130)	126	135
Minimum frontal breadth (9)	-	-	94	92	-	-	-	-
Maximum frontal breadth (10)	114	(108)	113	118	103	-	-	111
Bi-auricular breadth (11)	(110)	111	108	115	-	(112)	-	-
Greatest occipital breadth (12)	100	(96)	104	96	101	(107)	100	112
Bi-mastoid breadth (13)	-	(104)	102	121	-	-	-	-
Basion-bregma height (17)	-	-	126	-	-	(125)	-	-
Basion vertex height, total height of skull (17-2)	-	-	134	-	-	(128)	-	-
Auriculo bregmatic height (20)	(124)	125	120	127	-	(115)	(123)	127
Porion (auriculo) vertex height (21)	(125)	126	122	132	-	(118)	(126)	129
Calvarial height (22)	110	103	106	108	-	92	157	-
Lambda calvarial height (22b)	171	(173)	180	172	172	(176)	173	-
Frontal perpendicular height [22e]	31	31	24	24	-	(30)	29	-
Parietal perpendicular height [22f]	19	18	24	22	-	(13)	23	-
Occipital perpendicular height [22g]	25	25	-	-	-	(33)	-	-
Horizontal circumference of skull (23)	(495)	(500)	515	500	490	(500)	-	-
Transverse arc (24b)	(310)	300	290	300	-	(285)	-	
Longitudinal arc (25)	-	(370)	365		-	(360)	-	-
Frontal arc (26)	130	135	125	130	-	(125)	120	-
Parietal arc (27)	115	(130)	125	125	120	(125)	130	130
Occipital arc (28)	-	(105)	115		-	(110)	-	-
Frontal chord (29)	113	115	112	116	-	(102)	107	-
Parietal chord (30)	103	(119)	113	111	111	(113)	120	119
Occipital chord (31)	-	(85)	96		-	(93)	-	-
Facial length, facial depth (40)	-	-	104	-	-	-	-	-
Lateral facial length (41)	68	-	73	70	-	(70)	-	-
Lower facial length, inferior facial depth (42)	-	-	-	-	-	-	-	-

Specimen number	02	14	18	20	23	26	32	34
Age	50+ y	20- 25 y	40-45 y	35-40 y	18-20 y	40-45 y	18-19 y	Adult
Sex	F	M	F	F	F	F	F	F?
Outer bi-orbital breadth, upper facial breadth (43)	-	-	106	100	-	-	-	-
Inner bi-orbital breadth (43-1)	-	-	97	90	-	-	-	-
Bi-orbital breadth (44)	-	-	99	97	94	-	-	-
Bi-zygomatic breadth (45)	-	-	120	120	-	(111)	-	-
Breadth of upper jaw (46)	-	-	97	97	88	(85)	-	-
Morphological facial height (47)	-		-	110	-	-	-	-
Upper facial height, morphological superior facial ht. (48)	65	66	74	63	61	-	-	-
Breadth of nasal root, posterior inter-orbital breadth (49)	-	-	26	-	-	-	-	-
Anterior inter-orbital breadth (50)	23	-	24	22	19	(22)	-	-
Orbital breadth (51), right left	(40) -	-	42 41	43 (40)	40 42	- (41)	-	-
Orbital height (52), right Left	(38) -	-	36 36	33 (32)	- 33	- (37)	-	-
Nasal breadth (54)	(25)	(23)	(27)	(25)	28	(23)	-	-
Nasal height (55)	(46)	(53)	(53)	47	47	(43)	-	-
Length of Nasal bones (56)	(19)	28	(22)	-	23	(19)	-	-
Maxillo-alveolar length, length of upper jaw (60)	-		65	-	-	-	-	-
Maxillo-alveolar breadth, breadth of upper jaw (61)	(62)		69	-	-	(62)	-	-
Sub-nasal height (48-1)	(29)	(20)	(31)	(21)	22	-	-	-
Palatal length (62)	-		57	-	-	-	-	-
Palatal breadth (63)	-		40	-	-	(39)	-	-
Palatal height (64)	-		19	-	-	(14)	-	-
External palatal arc (80)	130		155	-	-	-	-	-
Molar teeth row length (80-3), right Left	27 28	- 22 (2nd)	35 21(2nd)	(32) -	-	- -	-	-
Premolar teeth row length [80-3a], right left	15 16	16 -	18 16	(15) -	16	- -	-	-
Bi-condylar breadth (65)	(106)	(103)	-	113	-	-	-	-
Bi-coronoid breadth (65-1)	(84)	(87)	-	94	-	-	-	-
Bi-gonial breadth (66)	(89)	(80)	-	93	-	-	-	-

Specimen number	02	14	18	20	23	26	32	34
Age	50+ y	20- 25 y	40-45 y	35-40 y	18-20 y	40-45 y	18-19 y	Adult
Sex	F	M	F	F	F	F	F	F?
Bi-mental breadth, anterior breadth (67)	-	-	-	-	-	-	-	-
Length of lower jaw (68)	(85)	(80)	-	99	-	-	-	-
Condylo-symphyseal length (68-1), right Left	(121) (122)	(122) (120)	-	121 116	-	-	-	-
Chin height, symphyseal height (69)	(37)	(30)	-	31	-	-	-	-
Condylar height, height of ascending ramus (70), right left	(68) (62)	(56) (65)	-	66 55	- 53	-	-	-
Height of coronoid (70-1), right left	(67) (62)	(62) (61)	-	60 58	- 54	-	-	-
Ascending ramus minimum breadth (71), right left	(34) -	(33) (35)	-	33 30	- 31	-	-	-
Ascending ramus maximum breadth (71-1), right left	(37) -	(35) (35)	-	35 32	- 33	-	-	-
Condylo-coronoid breadth, right left	(34) (40)	(41) (38)	-	33 28	- 31	-	-	-
External mandibular arc (80a)	(190)	(190)	-	195	-	-	-	-
Molar teeth row length [80-1a], right Left	(35) (38)	- (35)	-	-	-	-	-	-
Premolar teeth row length [80-b], right left	(12) (14)	- (16)	-	-	- 15	-	-	-
Total profile angle, facial profile angle (72)	84 (Meso-p-rog-na-th-ous)	77.5 (pro-gnath-ous)	77.5 (pro-gnath-ous)	83 (Meso-prog-nath-ous)	-	-	-	-
Nasal profile angle (73)	88.5 (Otho-gnat-hous)	84 (Meso-gnath-ous)	84 (Meso-gnath-ous)	82 (Meso-gnath-ous)	-	-	-	-
Alveolar profile angle (74)	71 (Pro-gnath-ous)	64 (Hyper-progna-thus)	66 (Hyper-progna-thus)	85.5 (Ortho-gna-thous)	-	-	-	-

Specimen number	02	14	18	20	23	26	32	34
Age	50+ y	20- 25 y	40-45 y	35-40 y	18-20 y	40-45 y	18-19 y	Adult
Sex	F	M	F	F	F	F	F	F?
Profile angle of nasal root (75)	79	77	51.5	74	-	73	-	-
Metopic angle, profile angle of forehead (32)	85	81.5	71.5	85	-	81	-	-
Lambda-opisthion angle (33)	-	60	59	-	-	61	-	-
Inclination angle of foramen magnum (34)	-	-	15	-	-	12	-	-
Calvarial base angle (37)	13	11	13	6.5	-	11	-	-
Glabella-inion angle	3	4	4	3.5	-	2	-	-
Nasion-basion angle	-	-	12	-	-	19	-	-
Lambda-inion angle	85.5	90	88	96	-	75	-	-
Bregma angle of Schwalbe (32-1)	63	58.5	61	59.5	-	59.5	-	-
Lambda angle of Schwalbe (33- 1a)	86	90.5	88	96	-	75.5	-	-
Angles of superior facial triangle N - ba - pr Ba - pr - n Pr - n - ba	- - -	34 83 63	41 66.5 72.5		-	-	-	-
	-	34	41	-	-	-	-	-
	-	83	66.5	-	-	-	-	-
	-	63	72.5	-	-	-	-	-
Angles of cranial quadrilateral L – ba - n Ba- n - b N - b - l B – l - ba					-	-	-	-
	-	89	109	-	-	107	-	-
	-	87	76	-	-	87	-	-
	-	103	105	-	-	107	-	-
	-	81	70	-	-	69	--	-

Table 5.2b: Cranial indices on Farmana individuals from 2 to 34

Specimen number	02	14	18	20	23	26	32	34
Age	50+ y	20- 25 y	40-45 y	35-40 y	18-20 y	40-45 y	18-19 y	Adult
Sex	F	M	F	F	F	F	F	F?
Cranial capacity (Lee-Pearson 1901) (38)	-	-	1256.8	-	-	1280.97	-	-
Cranial index (I 1)	70 (Ortho-cranial)	68.30 (Hyper-dolicho-cranial	66.8 (Hyper-dolicho-cranial)	74.5 (Dolicho-cranial)	-	70.3 (Dolicho-cranial)	70.4 (Dolicho-cranial)	-

Specimen number	02	14	18	20	23	26	32	34
Age	50+ y	20- 25 y	40-45 y	35-40 y	18-20 y	40-45 y	18-19 y	Adult
Sex	F	M	F	F	F	F	F	F?
Length-height cranial index, vertical index (I 2)	-	-	68.4 (Camae-cranial)	-	-	67.6 (Cham-aecra-nial)	-	-
Breadth-height cranial index, trans. Vertical index (I 3)	-	-	102.4 (Acro-cranial)	-	-	96.1 (Metrio-cranial)	-	-
Auriculo-vertical index (I 4)	70 (Hypsi-cranial)	68.3 (Hypsi-cranial)	65.2 (Hypsi-cranial)	71.7 (Hypsi-cranial)	-	62.1 (Ortho-cranial)	68.7 (Hyps-icranial)	-
Calvarial height-breadth index (I 6)	88.7	82.4	86.1	81.8	-	-	-	-
Hauschild`s circumference height index (I 9)	-	-	24.4		-	25	-	-
Sagittal arc index (I 10)	-	33.7	32.8		-	31.9	-	-
Transverse frontal index (I 12)	-	-	83.1	78	-	-	-	-
Transverse fronto breadth index, frontal index (I 13)	-	-	76.4 (Eury-metopic)	69.6 (Eury-metopic)	-	-	-	-
Skull modulus (I 37)	-	-	144.3		-	146.6	-	-
Total facial index (I 38)	-	-	-	91.6 (Lepto-prosopic)	-	-	-	-
Jugo-mandibular index (I 40)	-	-	-	77.5	-	-	-	-
Jugo-malar index (I 41)	-	-	80.8	80.8	-	76.6	-	-
Kollman`s upper facial index (I 39)	-	-	66.6 (Hyper-lepten)	55 (Lep-ton)	-	-	-	-
Orbital index (I 42), right left	95 (Hypso-conch) -	-	85.7 (Hypsi-conch) 87.8 (Hypsi-conch)	76.7 (Meso-conch) 80 (Meso-conch)	- 78.6 (Meso-conch)	- 90.24 (Hypsi-conch)	- -	-
Nasal index (I 48)	54.3 (Cham-aerhine)	43.3 (Lepto-rhine)	52.9 (Cham-aerhine)	53.2 (Cham-aerhine)	53.1 (Chama-erhine)	53.4 (Cham-aerhine)	-	-
Maxillo-alveolar index, Palato-alveolar index (I 54)	-	-	106.1 (Doli-churanic)		-	-	-	-
Mandibular index (I 62)	80.2 (Dolicho-steno-mandibu-lar)	-	-	87.6 (Dolicho-steno-mandibu-lar)	-	-	-	-

Specimen number	02	14	18	20	23	26	32	34
Age	50+ y	20- 25 y	40-45 y	35-40 y	18-20 y	40-45 y	18-19 y	Adult
Sex	F	M	F	F	F	F	F	F?
Gonio-condylar index (I 64)	83	77.67	-	82.3	-	-	-	-
Transverse cranio-facial index (I 71)	-	-	97.5	90.9	-	85.4	-	-
Jugo-frontal index (I 73)	-	-	78.3	76.6	-	-	-	-

Table 5.3a: Craniometric observations on Farmana individuals from 45 to 67

Specimen number	45	52	53	62	66	67
Age	13-15 y	3.5 y	30 y	15 y	50 y	35 y
Sex	NA	NA	F	F?	M	M
Maximum cranial length (1)	173	167	188	188	176	(192)
Glabella inion length (2)	168	155	186	185	174	(187)
Glabella lambda length (3)	169	163	188	183	170	(184)
Maximum cranial breadth (8)		127	118	117	135	-
Minimum frontal breadth (9)	85	88	-	94	-	(86)
Maximum frontal breadth (10)	104	108	107	106	114	-
Bi-auricular breadth (11)	-	-	-	-	-	-
Greatest occipital breadth (12)	98	106	86	97	104	-
Bi-mastoid breadth (13)	-	-	-	-	-	-
Basion-bregma height (17)	-	115	-	127	128	-
Basion vertex height, total height of skull (17-2)	-	117	-	133	129	-
Auriculo bregmatic height (20)	-	116	-	121	118	(132)
Porion (auriculo) vertex height(21)	-	121	-	130	120	(138)
Calvarial height (22)	-	100	-	101	101	(105)
Lambda calvarial height (22b)	167	147	186	183	170	(182)
Frontal perpendicular height [22e]	25	24	28	27	22	-
Parietal perpendicular height [22f]	23	26	25	27	27	-
Occipital perpendicular height [22g]	-	29	-	28	27	-
Horizontal circumference of skull (23)	470	480	520	510	-	-
Transverse arc (24b)	-	285	-	-	-	-
Longitudinal arc (25)	-	355	-	380	350	(360)
Frontal arc (26)	115	120	135	130	115	(140)
Parietal arc (27)	135	115	135	140	130	(130)
Occipital arc (28)	-	120	-	110	105	(90)
Frontal chord (29)	114	104	115	115	104	(123)
Parietal chord (30)	119	103	130	120	118	(121)
Occipital chord (31)	-	100	-	92	90	(87)
Facial length, facial depth (40)	-	-	-	-	-	-
Lateral facial length (41)	-	-	-	-	-	(72)
Lower facial length, inferior facial depth (42)	-	-	-	-	-	-
Outer bi-orbital breadth, upper facial breadth (43)	-	-	-	-	-	-
Inner bi-orbital breadth (43-1)	-	-	-	-	-	-

Specimen number	**45**	**52**	**53**	**62**	**66**	**67**
Age	**13-15 y**	**3.5 y**	**30 y**	**15 y**	**50 y**	**35 y**
Sex	**NA**	**NA**	**F**	**F?**	**M**	**M**
Bi-orbital breadth (44)	-	-	-	-	-	(87)
Bi-zygomatic breadth (45)	-	-	-	-	-	(99)
Breadth of upper jaw (46)	-	-	-	-	-	95
Morphological facial height (47)	-	-	-	-	-	-
Upper facial height, morphological superior facial ht. (48)	-	-	-	-	-	68
Breadth of nasal root, posterior inter-orbital breadth (49)	-	-	-	-	-	-
Anterior inter-orbital breadth (50)	-	-	22	21	-	(22)
Orbital breadth (51), right left	- 40	- 34	45 -	- -	39 -	(33) (34)
Orbital height (52), right Left	37 34	- 30	37 -	- 34	35 -	(29) (29)
Nasal breadth (54)	-	-	-	25	-	(28)
Nasal height (55)	-	-	-	47	-	(48)
Length of Nasal bones (56)	22	-	-	-		(21)
Maxillo-alveolar length, length of upper jaw (60)	-	-	-	-	-	-
Maxillo-alveolar breadth, breadth of upper jaw (61)	-	-	-	61	-	-
Sub-nasal height (48-1)	-	-	-	37	-	21
Palatal length (62)	-	-	-	-	-	-
Palatal breadth (63)	-	-	-	-	-	-
Palatal height (64)	-	-	-	-	-	-
External palatal arc (80)	-	-	-	-	-	(125)
Molar teeth row length (80-3), right Left	-	-	-	-	-	24 (2nd) 22 (2nd)
Premolar teeth row length [80-3a], right left	-	-	-	-	-	19 15
Bi-condylar breadth (65)	-	-	-	-	-	-
Bi-coronoid breadth (65-1)	-	-	-	-	-	-
Bi-gonial breadth (66)	-	-	-	-	-	-
Bi-mental breadth, anterior breadth (67)	-	-	-	-	-	-
Length of lower jaw (68)	-	-	-	-	-	90
Condylo-symphyseal length (68-1), right Left	-	-	-	-	-	116 122
Chin height, symphyseal height (69)	-	-	-	-	-	(36)
Condylar height, height of ascending ramus (70), right left	-	-	-	-	-	(55) 59
Height of coronoid (70-1), right left	-	-	-	-	-	(61) (60)
Ascending ramus minimum breadth (71), right left	-	-	-	-	-	33 30

Specimen number	45	52	53	62	66	67
Age	13-15 y	3.5 y	30 y	15 y	50 y	35 y
Sex	NA	NA	F	F?	M	M
Ascending ramus maximum breadth (71-1), right left	-	-	-	-	-	39 33
Condylo-coronoid breadth, right left	-	-	-	-	-	- -
External mandibular arc (80a)	-	-	-	-	-	-
Molar teeth row length [80-1a], right Left	-	-	-	-	-	-
Premolar teeth row length [80-b], right left	-	-	-	-	-	-
Total profile angle, facial profile angle (72)	-	-	-	-	-	84 (Mesoprognathus)
Nasal profile angle (73)	-	-	-	-	-	86.5 (Othognathus)
Alveolar profile angle (74)	-	-	-	-	-	79 (Prognathus)
Profile angle of nasal root (75)	-	-	-	-	-	77
Metopic angle, profile angle of forehead (32)	-	84	--	85	85	84
Lambda-opisthion angle (33)	-	55.5	-	51	57	(80)
Inclination angle of foramen magnum (34)	-	7	-	-	9.5	(20)
Calvarial base angle (37)	-	10	-	9	11.5	5
Glabella-inion angle	-	2.5	-	2	9.5	2
Nasion-basion angle	-	32.5	-	28	27	(25)
Lambda-inion angle	-	101	-	102	102	78.5
Bregma angle of Schwalbe (32-1)	-	65	-	57	6.1	59
Lambda angle of Schwalbe (33- 1a)	-	88.5	-	93	89.5	78.5
Angles of superior facial triangle N - ba - pr Ba - pr - n Pr - n - ba	-	-	-	-	-	 (31) (88) (61)
Angles of cranial quadrilateral L – ba - n Ba- n - b N - b - l B – l - ba	- - - - 	 104 88 100 68	- - - - -	 113.5 78.5 104.5 65.5	 112 76.5 101.5 70	 (99) (83) (90) (88)

Table 5.3b: Cranial indices on Farmana individual from 45 to 67

Specimen number	45	52	53	62	66	67
Age	**13-15 y**	**3.5 y**	**30 y**	**15 y**	**50 y**	**35 y**
Sex	**NA**	**NA**	**F**	**F?**	**M**	**M**
Cranial capacity (Lee-Pearson 1901) (38)	-	-	-	-	-	-
Cranial index (I 1)	-	76.04 (Meso-ranial)	62.76 (Ultra-dolicho-cranial)	62.2 (Uultra-dolicho-cranial)	76.7 (Meso-ranial)	-
Length-height cranial index, vertical index (I 2)	-	68.9 (Cham-aecranial)	-	67.5 (Cham-aecra-nial	72.7 (Orth-ocranial)	-
Breadth-height cranial index, trans. Vertical index (I 3)	-	90.5 (Tapei-no-cranial)	-	107.6 (Acrocranial)	94.8 (Me-trio-cranial)	-
Auriculo-vertical index (I 4)	-	69.4 (Hypsicranial)	-	64.3 (Hypsicranial)	67 (Hypsicranial)	-
Calvarial height-breadth index (I 6)	-	78.7	-	84.8	74.8	68.75 (Hypsicranial)
Hauschild`s circumference height index (I 9)	-	23.9	-	24.9	-	-
Sagittal arc index (I 10)	-	32.7	-	31.8	33.7	-
Transverse frontal index (I 12)	82.5	80	-	88.6	-	36.66
Transverse fronto breadth index, frontal index (I 13)	-	69.3 (Eu-ryme-topic)	-	80.34 (Eu-rome-topic)	-	-
Skull modulus (I 37)	-	136.3	-	144	146.3	-
Total facial index (I 38)	-		-	-	-	-
Jugo-mandibular index (I 40)	-	-	-	-	--	-
Jugo-malar index (I 41)	-	-	-	-	-	-
Kollman`s upper facial index (I 39)	-	-	-	-	-	95.95
Orbital index (I 42), right left	- 85 (Long Orbit)	- 88.2 (Long Orbit)	82.2 (Mesoconch) -	-	89.7 (Long Orbit) -	68.7 (Hyperlepten)
Nasal index (I 43)	-	-	-	53.1 (Broad Nose)	-	87.8 (hypsiconch) 85.3 (hypsiconch)
Maxillo-alveolar index, Palato-alveolar index (I 54)	-	-	-	-	-	58.3 (Very Broad nose)
Mandibular index (I 62)	-	-	-	-	-	-
Gonio-condylar index (I 64)	-	-	-	-	-	-
Transverse cranio-facial index (I 71)	-	-	-	-	-	-
Jugo-frontal index (I 73)	-	-	-	-	-	-
						86.86

Table 5.4a: Comparison of cranial measurements of male specimens from Farmana to other sites (*: only one specimen)

Measurement (M.S.code)	Neva-sa	Kaothe	Daima-bad	Inamg-aon	Chand-oli	Harappa R 37	Harappa Area G	Harappa H-1	Harappa H-II	Mohen-Jo daro	Burza-hom	Pikli-hal	Hulli-kallu	Ieej	Farmana
Frequency	1	1	1	1a	1	13	7	3	5	3	1a	1	1	1	2
Measurements															
Maximum cranial length (1)	172	175	194	181	197	188	181	187	189	197	190	172	172	179	185
Maximum cranial breadth (8)	138	129	133	138	128	133	138	138	145	130	133	139	144	145	130
Basion bregma height (17)	--	129	145	137	--	134	134	135	135	139	140	141	142	--	128*
Auriculo vertex height (21)	130	111	138	121	--	115	114	119	119	122	126	--	117	107	123
Auriculo-bregma height (20)	130	108	135	119	126	115	114	118	119	--	--	124	116	105	121
Minimum frontal diameter (9)	98	96	89	87	81	95	99	97	96	95	97	95	94	97	--
Bizygomatic diameter (45)	128	135	121	122	--	131	128	133	136	127	134	126	124	--	--
Prosthion-nasion height (48)	69	56	--	65	--	71	67	65	70	69	74	66	68	--	66*
Basion-nasion length (5)	--	97	--	101	--	--	--	--	--	99	110	103	99	--	--
Basion-prosthion length (40)	--	92	--	102	--	102	95	103	97	102	100	100	92	--	--
Nasal height (55)	48	44	--	46	--	51	51	49	53	46	55	45	46	--	53*
Nasal breadth (54)	25	24	--	22	--	27	26	27	26	22	28	23	25	--	23*
Orbital height (52)	36	32	40	31	--	34	31	32	33	31	36	35	33	--	35*
Orbital breadth (51)	41	41	--	36	--	42	41	41	41	37	40	45	40	--	39*
Bi-condylar breadth (65)	-	112	114	130	121	104	120	111	113	116	117	117	108	108	103*

Measurement (M.S.code)	Neva-sa	Kaothe	Daima-bad	Inamg-aon	Chand-oli	Harappa R 37	Harappa Area G	Harappa H-1	Harappa H-II	Mohen-Jo daro	Burza-hom	Pikli-hal	Hulli-kallu	Ieej	Farmana
Bi-gonial breadth (66)	96	99	96	90	92	89	91	87	79	102	84	93	95	112	80*
Symphyseal height (69)	33	30	39	34	29	34	31	29	30	35	33	35	30	29	30*
Ascending ramus height (70)	--	51	62	58	67	68	57	62	62	62	67	66	55	58	60*
Min.br.asce. ramus (71)	37	33	32	37	35	34	33	35	35	37	30	35	34	31	34*
Con.-symphyseal lgt (68/1)	--	114	108	103	--	--	--	--	--	--	77	--	120	129	121
Mandibular length (68)	80	72	79	72	--	82	79	84	87	81	68	--	75	75	--
Mandibular angle (79)	135	121	124	121	116	120	119	121	111	117	115	124	121	125	--

Table 5.4b: Comparison of cranial Indices of male specimens from Farmana to other sites (*: only one specimen)

Index (M.S. code)	Nev-asa	Kao-the	Daim-abad	Inam-gaon	Chan-doli	Hara-ppa R-37	Hara-ppa Area G	Hara-ppa H-I	Hara-ppa H-II	Mohen-jo-daro	Burza-hom	Pikli-hal	Hulli-kallu	Ieej	Farm-ana
Frequency	1	1	1	1a	1	13	7	3	5	3	1a	1	1	1	2
Indices															
Cranial capacity (38)	--	1299.2	1519.8	1444.3	1519	1387.5	1387.7	1470.8	1505.1	1471.5b	1465.7b	1421.3b	1460.1	--	---
Cranial Index (I 1)	80.2	73.7	68.6	76.2	65	71.1	76.4	73.8	76.7	66	70	80.8b	83.7	81	72.5
Cranial module (I 37)	--	144.3	157.3	152	--	151.5	150.7	154.6	156.1	155.7	154.3b	150.7b	152.7	--	146.3*
Total facial index (I 38)	89.8	77.4	--	--	--	93.6	93.0b	93.8	85.6	88.9	91	97.6b	89.5	--	--
Upper facial index (I 39)	53.9	41.5	--	53.3	--	52.6	51.6	49.1	50	53.9	55.2	52.4	54.8	--	--
Height (au-v) length index	75.6	63.4	71.1	66.9	--	61.3	63.1	63.6b	63.0b	61.9b	66.3	--	68	59.8	--
Height (au-v) breadth index	94.2	86	103.8	87.7	--	86.2	82	86.2b	82.1b	93.8b	94.7	--	81.3	73.8	--
Height (ba-b) length index (I 2)	--	73.7	74.7	75.7	--	71.3b	74.0b	72.2b	71.4b	70.6	73.7	82.0b	82.6	--	72.7*

Index (M.S. code)	Nev-asa	Kao-the	Daim-abad	Inam-gaon	Chan-doli	Hara-ppa R-37	Hara-ppa Area G	Hara-ppa H-I	Hara-ppa H-II	Mohen-jo-daro	Burza-hom	Pikli-hal	Hulli-kallu	Ieej	Farm-ana
Height (ba-b) brea. index (I 3)	--	100	109	99.3	--	100.8b	97.1b	97.8b	93.1b	107.2	105.3	101.4b	98.6	--	94.8*
Height (au-b) length index (I 4)	75.6	61.7	69.6	65.8	63.9	61.3	63.1	62.1	63.0b	--	--	72.1b	67.4	58.7	67.65
Height (au-b) br. index (I 6)	94.2	83.7	101.5	86.2	98.4	86.2	82	85.9	82.1b	--	--	87.9b	80.6	72.4	78.6
Zygo-frontal index (I 73)	76.5	71.1	--	71.3	--	71.3	77.9	72.9b	70.6b	74.8b	72.4b	75.4b	75.8	--	--
Nasal index (I 48)	52	54.6	--	47.8	--	50.6	50.6	55.2	47.6	47.8b	50.9	51.1	54.4	--	43.3*
Orbital index (I 42)	87.8	78	--	86.1	--	80.8	78.5	80.0b	79.2	84.5	90	77.8	82.5	--	89.7*
Mandibular index (I 62)	--	64.3	69.3	55.4	--	78.8b	65.8b	75.7b	77.0b	69.8b	58.1	--	69.4	69.4	--
Jugo-mandibular index (I 40)	75	73.3	79.3	73.8	--	69.7	75.6	65.5	55.5	80.3b	62.7b	73.8	76.6	--	--

Table 5.5a: Comparison of cranial measurements of female specimens from Farmana to other sites (*: only one specimen)

Measurement (M.S. code)	Nevasa	Kaothe	Inamgaon	Harappa R-37	Harappa Area G	Harappa H-I	Harappa H-II	Mohen-jo-daro	Burza-hom	Pikli-hal	Langh-naj	Tekkala-kota	Farmana
Frequency	1	1	1a	15	2	11	2	1	1a	1	1	1a	3
Maximum cranial length (1)	173	--	183	180	174	176	182	180	190	175	190	181	182
Maximum cranial breadth (8)	132	137	137	131	130	132	133	--	129	131	136	122	128
Basion-bregma height (17)	135	130	136	128	125	126	134	--	--	131	--	---	125
Auriculo-vertex height (21)	125	116	115	111	108	108	109	--	120	--	--	--	124
Auriculo-bregma height (20)	122	113	113	--	--	--	--	--	--	110	-117	114	120
Minimum frontal diameter (9)	94	--	100	93	89	91	93	--	97	94	95	84	93
Bi-zygomatic diameter (45)	105	124	-118	125	116	121	117	--	132	128	--	--	117

Measurement (M.S. code)	Nevasa	Kaothe	Inamgaon	Harappa R-37	Harappa Area G	Harappa H-I	Harappa H-II	Mohen-jo-daro	Burza-hom	Pikli-hal	Langh-naj	Tekkala-kota	Farmana
Prosthion-nasion height (48)	60	--	-65	65	66	59	66	--	70	--	--	72	68
Basion-nasion length (5)	--	--	102	--	--	--	--	--	--	--	--	--	--
Basion-prosthion length (40)	--	90	-95	94	92	94	100	--	--	--	--	--	104
Nasal height (55)	43	--	46	48	46	46	46	--	51	46	--	52	47
Nasal breadth (54)	-24	21	24	25	23	25	24	--	28	23	--	24	25
Orbital height (52)	31	--	32	34	31	32	33	36	39	33	--	35	35
Orbital breadth (51)	39	--	41	41	39	39	41	38	37	41	--	37	41
Bi-condylar breadth (65)	-108	116	109	108	--	--	111	--	119	--	--	-112	113*
Bi-gonial breadth (66)	97	90	82	81	--	86	84	--	87	--	-80	90	93*
Symphyseal height (69)	31	28	31	30	--	23	30	--	28	--	24	34	31*
Ascending ramus height (70)	--	52	43	59	--	52	58	--	55	--	49	58	60*
Min.br. ascending ramus (71)	32	29	34	32	--	32	32	--	33	--	28	38	31*
Cond.-symphy. length (68/1)	108	121	106	--	--	--	--	--	--	--	--	105	118*
Mandibular length (68)	74	78	--	75	--	82	75	--	69	--	--	--	99*
Mandibular angle (79)	125	130	134	119	--	126	123	--	124	--	--	115	--

Table 5.5b: Comparison of cranial indices of female specimens from Farmana to other sites

Index	Nevasa	Kaothe	Inam-gaon	Harappa R-37	Harappa Area G	Harappa H-I	Harappa H-II	Mohen-jo-daro	Burza-hom	Pikli-Hal	Langh-naj	Tekkala-kota	Farmana
Frequency	1	1	1a	15	2	11	2	1	1a	1	1	1a	1
Cranial capacity (38)	1292.92	--	1358.8	1285.3	1205.8	1235.4	1251.4	--	1413.3	1280.5	1430	1037.2	1268.88
Cranial Index (I 1)	76.3	--	74.8	72.6	74.5	75.8	76.1	--	67.9	74.9	71.6	67.4	70.5
Cranial module (I 37)	146.6	--	152	146.4	143	145.1	147.6	--	--	--	--	--	145.45
Total facial index (I 38)	95.2	--	94.1	89.6	--	--	96.5	--	87.8	--	--	--	91.6
Upper facial index (I 39)	57.1	--	55.1	52.2	56	51.4	54.8	--	53	--	--	--	60.8
Height (au-v) length index	72.2	--	62.8	85.2	61.6	60.2	62.6	--	63.2	--	--	--	--
Height (au-v) breadth index	94.6	84.7	83.9	61.9	82.7	81.8	82.3	--	93	--	--	--	--
Height (ba-b) length index (I 2)	78	--	74.3	71	71.3	77.1	76.9	--	--	74.9	--	--	68
Height (ba-b) brea. Index (I 3)	102.2	94.9	99.3	97.6	95.7	97.7	101.1	--	--	100	--	--	99.25
Height (au-b) length index (I 4)	70.52	--	61.7	--	--	--	--	--	--	62.9	61.6	63	66.3
Height (au-b) br. index (I 6)	94.4	82.5	82.5	--	--	--	--	--	--	84	86	93.4	83.95
Zygo-frontal index (I 73)	89.5	--	84.8	74.7	76.7	73.9	78.3	--	73.5	73.4	--	--	77.45
Nasal index (I 48)	55.8	--	52.2	51.6	51.4	55.1	53.3	--	54.5	50	--	46.2	55.16
Orbital index (I 42)	79.4	--	78.1	82.9	80.7	80.5	83	94.7	105.4	80.5	--	94.6	82.55
Mandibular index (I 62)	68.5	67.2	--	69.5	--	--	66.8	--	58	--	--	--	87.6
Jugo-mandibular index (I 40)	92.3	72.6	69.5	65	--	71.1	69.1	--	66	--	--	--	77.45

Craniometry Comparison of Farmana with other Sites

When the Farmana sample was compared with other crania from different Neolithic, Chalcolithic, Megalithic and other Harappan sites some interesting trends are noticed (Table 5.4a, 5.4b and 5.45 and 5.5b).

In Male crania the length and breadth graph, Farmana sample is placed at a different location in comparison with Harappa. The values of Farmana are close to Kaothe specimen. There is a close relation between Burzahom, Harappa R 37 and Daimabad. Nevasa and Piklihal are very close to each other in relation to length-breadth values. Rests of the points are comparatively far from each other (Fig. 5.2).

After comparing Total Facial Index with Upper Facial Index the Farmana male is close to Burzahom, Hulikallu, Mohenjo-daro, and Nevasa. Interestingly Harappa H-II is placed separately like Kaothe. Harappa R 37 and Harappa Area G is close to each other than Harappa H-I (Fig. 5.3).

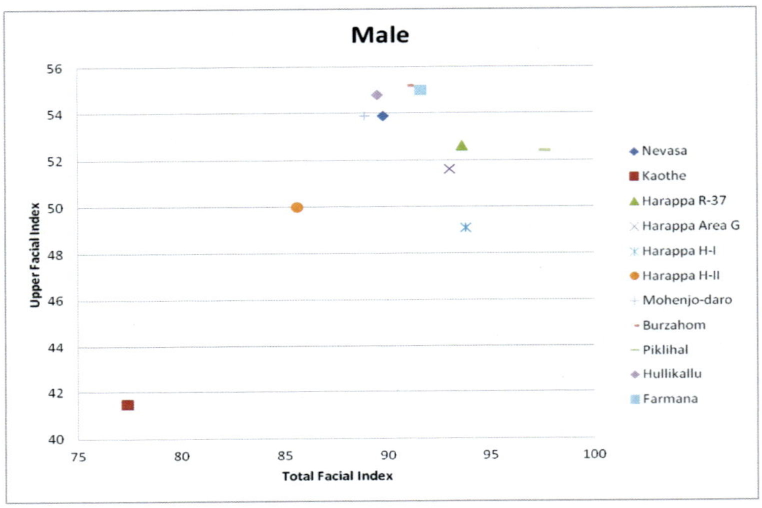

Figure 5.2: Comparison of Farmana male maximum cranial length and breadth to other sites

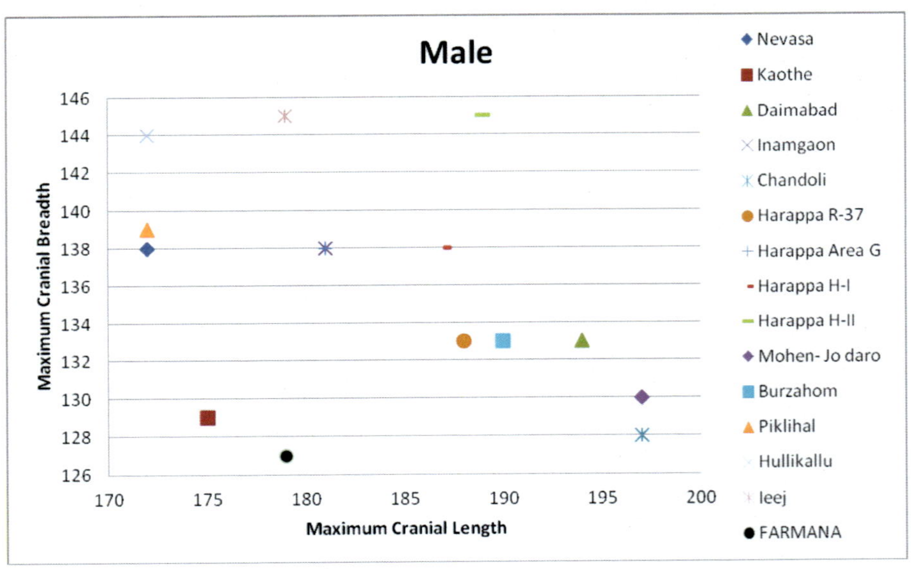

Figure 5.3: Comparison of the Farmana male total facial index to upper facial index to other sites

If we compare the female cranial length-breadth values of Farmana and Tekkalakota they are close to each other and Nevasa, Piklihal, Harappa H-1 and Harappa Area G are grouped together with near proximity of Harappa R 37 and Harappa H-II (Fig. 5.4). When cranial capacity and cranial Index are plotted on the graph Farmana women are away from the rest of the population. Sites like Nevasa, Harappa H-I, Harappa H-II, Harappa Area G are grouped together. Tekkalakota and Burzahom are placed separately from Farmana in contrast to the length and breadth values where Tekkalkota and Farmana are placed closed (Fig. 5.5).

When compare total facial index with the upper facial index the Farmana values are away from rest of the female population. Values for Nevasa, Inamgaon and Harappa H II are close together and Burzahome and Harappa R 37 are forming a group (Fig. 5.6).

It is interesting that in both cranial capacity and cranial index and facial index, both total and upper, the Farmana female are separate indicating some local elements. But it is very difficult to format some hypothesis about a population-based on few parameters.

The males are giving a contradictory picture as total and upper facial indices are close to some Neolithic-Chalcolithic population than to any Harappan population, except Mohenjo-Daro. In length -breadth indices it is again close to Chalcolithic specimen than that of Harappans.

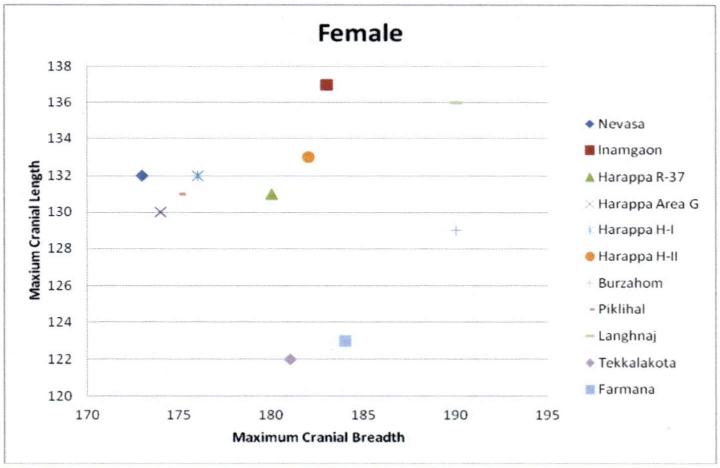

Figure 5.4: Comparison of Farmana female maximum cranial length and breadth to other sites

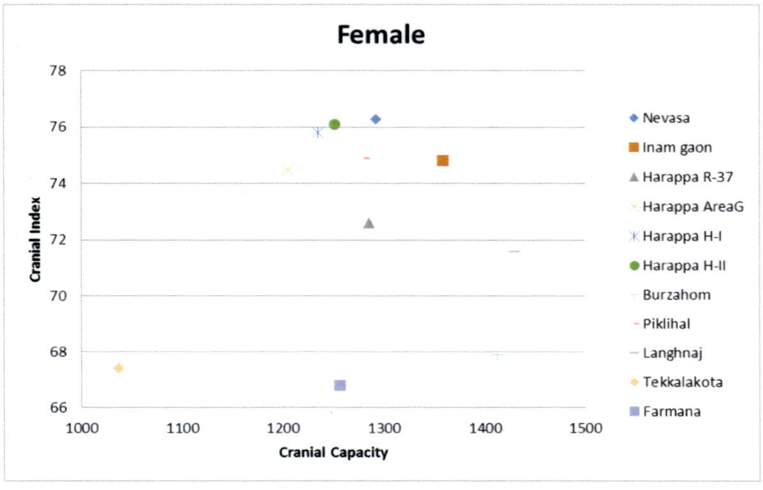

Figure 5.5: Comparison of Farmana cranial capacity and cranial Index to other sites

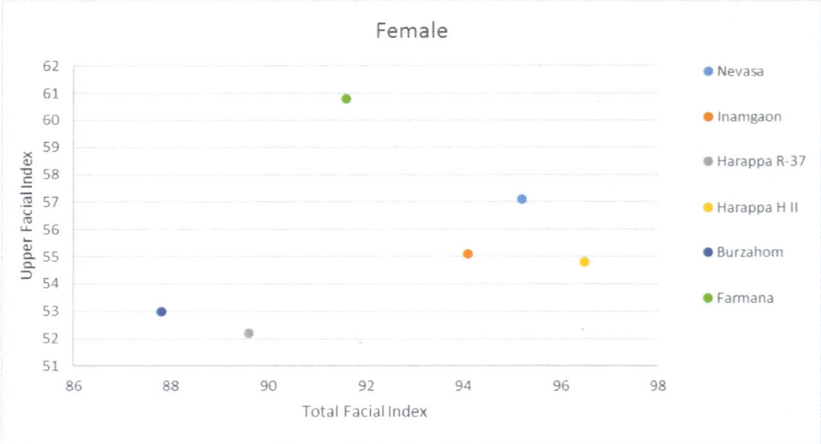

Figure 5.6: Comparison of Farmana female total facial index to upper facial index to other sites

Osteometry

Long bone measurements were possible only for few individuals and for few bones as well. The possible measurements are listed in the Table 5.6. Stature estimation was calculated using complete or almost complete and intact long bones, follows the method of Trotter (1970), where racially specific equations for White populations are used. The estimated values are being given in the bracket. Out of 35, long bone length is possible for seventeen individuals which allowed for calculating stature (Table 5.7). Out of seventeenn, ten individuals long bone lengths were estimated in the field when bones were *insitu*. There are nine females and eight males. The average male stature is 173.03 (in the range from 163.30 to 187.44) and for females, it is 166.07 (in the range from 157.22 to 177.63). In male individuals, skeleton 25 is tallest and in females, individual 11 is tallest.

Table 5.6: Long bone measurements

Spe. No	Age	Sex	Bone	Side	Anterior-Posterior (in mm)	Medio-Lateral (in mm)	Girth (in mm)	Length (in cm)
1	18-20	male	Femur	L	(26)	(24)	(80)	-
2	40-45	male	Femur	?	32	29	95	-
6	40-45	Female	Humerus	L	22	16	65	32
8	Adult	male	Femur	R	32	29	90	-
			Tibia	R	-	32	-	39
10	Adult	Male	Femur	R	25	29	91	41
			Tibia	R	-	29	-	-
			Tibia	L	-	28	-	-
			Humerus	L	20	(21)	(60)	-
			Humerus	R	(20)	(26)	(76)	-
			Ulna	R?	15	17	49	-

Spe. No	Age	Sex	Bone	Side	Anterior-Posterior (in mm)	Medio-Lateral (in mm)	Girth (in mm)	Length (in cm)
14	25		Femur	L	32	31	95	-
			Femur	R	(29)	(29)	(86)	-
			Tibia	L		33		-
			Humerus	R	17	20	60	-
25	Adult	male	Femur	R	39	-	-	-
			Femur	L	-	28	-	-
			Tibia	R	(25)	(38)	102	-
48	20±5		Femur	R	26	25	80	-
				L	27	23	80	-
64	20±5		Humerus	L	-	20	-	-
			Ulna	L	16	17	51	-
			Radius	L	13	15	45	-
			Femur	R	30	29	95	-
				L	31	30	99	-
			Tibia	R	(32)	-	-	-
				L	34	-	-	-
67	35		Humerus	L	22	18	61	-
			Femur	R	31	25	87	-
				L	30	26	88	-
			Tibia	R	31	24	88	-
				L	(31)	-	-	-
20	35-40		Humerus	R	(16)	(22)	(60)	-
				L	23	17	63	-
			Radius	R	12	14	40	-
			Ulna	R	-	16	-	-
			Femur	R	27	29	87	-
			Tibia	L	30	24	84	-
				R	31	23	83	-
			Fibula	L	13	11	37	-

Table 5.7: Stature estimation

Spe.No	Sex	Age	Bone	Side	Length measurement (cm)	Stature estimation (cm)	Mean value (cm)
8	Male	Adult	Femur	R	49	178.03±3.27	178.81
			Tibia	R	40	179.42±3.37	
			Femur+Tibia	R	89	178.99±2.99	
10	Female	Adult	Femur	R	41	155.37±3.72	157.22
			Tibia	R	33	160.23±3.66	
			Femur+Tibia	R	74	156.06±3.55	

Spe.No	Sex	Age	Bone	Side	Length measurement (cm)	Stature estimation (cm)	Mean value (cm)
11*	Female (?)	45±5	Tibia	L	39	177.63 ± 3.66	177.63
14*	Male	25	Humerus	R	32	169.01 ±4.05	178.18
			Radius	R	29	188.63 ±4.32	
			Ulna	R	30	185.05 ±4.32	
			Tibia	L	42	184.46 ±3.37	
18*	Female	40-45	Humerus	R	33	168.85±4.45	167.05
			Femur	R	45	165.25 ±3.72	
20	Female	35-40	Humerus	R	30	158.77±4.45	168.85
			Ulna	R	27	173.05±4.30	
			Tibia	L	38	174.73±3.66	
23*	Female	18-20	Tibia	L	30	151.53±3.66	151.53
25	Male	Adult	Femur	R	55	192.31±3.27	187.44
			Tibia	R	41	181.94±3.37	
			Femur+Tibia	R	96	188.09±2.99	
26*	Female	40-45	Humerus	L	34	172.21 ±4.45	172.02
			Tibia	L	37	171.83 ±3.66	
32	Female	18±1	Femur	R	46	167.72±3.72	170.80
			Tibia	L	38	174.73±3.66	
			Femur+Tibia	R+L	84	169.96±3.55	
48*	Male	20±5	Humerus	L	30	162.85 ±4.05	167.17
			Ulna	L	26	170.25 ±4.32	
			Femur	L	44	166.13 ±3.27	
			Tibia	L	36	169.34 ±3.37	
			Femur+Tibia	L	80	167.29 ±2.99	
50A*	Male	25	Tibia	R	34	164.30 ±3.37	164.30
53*	Female	30	Humerus	L	34	172.21 ±4.45	163.79
54*	Male	30	Humerus	R	31	165.93 ±4.05	163.30
			Ulna	R	24	162.85 ±4.32	
			Femur	R	42	161.37 ±3.27	
			Tibia	R	34	164.30 ±3.37	
			Femur+Tibia	R	76	162.09 ±2.99	
64	Male	20±5	Femur	R	46	170.89±3.27	173.86
			Tibia	L	39	176.90±3.37	
			Femur+Tibia	R+L	85	173.79±2.99	
65*	Female	30	Humerus	L	33	168.85 ±4.45	165.81
			Femur	R	44	162.78 ±3.72	
67	Male	35	Femur	L	48	175.65±3.27	171.22
			Tibia	R	37	166.82±3.37	
			Femur+Tibia	L+R	83	171.19±4.05	

* Measurements have been taken from field note

Dentition

Farmana is suffered from the bad preservation, even dentition not present completely. There are only 214 teeth available for study (Table 5.8). Many of them are broken or worn out. Some teeth are still attached to gnathic bones. Therefore, measurements and morphological observations are not possible even though they are present. Some teeth were sampled for isotopic analysis. Altogether 103 teeth (94 permanent and nine deciduous) were measured. Within 94 permanent teeth, eight teeth has only one measurement.

Table 5.8: Inventory of dentition preserved for analysis

Spe. No.	Total	Maxillary teeth	Mandibular teeth
1	1	1	-
2	32	16	16
5	2	2	-
6	5	-	5
11	2	-	2
14	24	13	11
15	2	2	-
18	21	14	7
20	30	14	16
23	22	14	8
26	2	2	-
41	5	4	1
45	11	5	6
47	6	5	1
52	11 (9 de.)	5	4 + 2 (per)
54	1	-	1
58	1	-	1
62	10	10	-
65	4	2	2
66	5	5	-
67	17	12	5
21 individuals	214 (11 dec + 203 per)	126	88

METRIC ANALYSIS

Methodology:

Two basic measurements have been carried out for each tooth following the Moorrees' (1957a, 1957b) technique. These consist of maximum crown length (mesio-distal diameter) and maximum crown breadth (bucco-lingual diameter). The mesio-distal diameter (MD) is the maximum dimension of the tooth crown in the mesio-distal direction, parallel to the occlusal and the labial surface. The bucco-lingual crown diameter (BL) is defined as the greatest distance between the buccal and the lingual surface of tooth crown in a plane perpendicular to that of the mesio-distal diameter. The crown measurements are carried out with electronic MAX-CAL digital caliper with an accuracy of 0.01 mm.

The primary comparative standard in the analysis of tooth size is the crown area (CA) or the cross-sectional area of the tooth. This figure of crown size is obtained by multiplying mesio-distal diameter by bucco-lingual diameter. The crown index (CI), a measure of crown shape is the ratio of mesio-distal and bucco-lingual diameter expressed in terms of percentage, as suggested by Wolpoff (1971). The measure of crown bulk, crown module (CM), is the average of mesio-distal and bucco-lingual values. The formulae used for calculating crown area, crown index and crown module are summarized below.

$$CA = MD \times BL$$

$$CI = MD \times 100 / BL$$

$$CM = (MD + BL) / 2$$

Due to fragmentary condition, no TCA or MCA values calculated for the Farmana specimens. Following are the measurements on deciduous (Table 5.9) and permanent teeth (Table 5.10 and 5.11) from maxilla and mandible. General traits are observed. For example, deciduous first molars are smaller in MD and BL diameter than second deciduous molars. For dm2s MD and BL diameter values are close to M1s. In both maxillary and mandibular dentition M1 is bigger than M2 and M3 is smaller in comparison to M2. Only in one case of specimen 14, mandibular LM2 is bigger than M1.

Table 5.9: Odonotometry of deciduous teeth

Tooth		Spe. 5				Spe. 52			
		Maxilla		Mandible		Maxilla		Mandible	
		R	L	R	L	R	L	R	L
di1	MD	-	-	-	-	-	5.48	-	-
	BL	-	-	-	-	-	4.53	-	-
	CA	-	-	-	-	-	24.82	-	-
	CI	-	-	-	-	-	120.97	-	-
	CM	-	-	-	-	-	5.00	-	-
Dc	MD	-	-	-	-	-	-	6.6	-
	BL	-	-	-	-	-	-	5.29	-
	CA	-	-	-	-	-	-	34.9	-
	CI	-	-	-	-	-	-	124.76	-
	CM	-	-	-	-	-	-	5.94	-
dm1	MD	-	-	-	-	6.34	6.53	8.80	
	BL	-	-	-	-	8.57	8.30	6.35	
	CA	-	-	-	-	54.33	54.19	55.88	
	CI	-	-	-	-	73.97	78.67	138.58	
	CM	-	-	-	-	7.45	7.41	7.57	
dm2	MD	9.41	-	-	-	9.92	10.22	-	10.54
	BL	8.66	-	-	-	9.68	8.97	-	8.74
	CA	81.49	-	-	-	96.02	91.67	-	92.11
	CI	108.66	-	-	-	102.47	113.93	-	120.59
	CM	9.03	-	-	-	9.8	9.59	-	9.64

Table 5.10: Odontometric data for Maxillary dentition

Tooth		Spe. 1		Spe. 14		Spe. 18		Spe. 23		Spe. 26		Sep. 41	
		R	L	R	L	R	L	R	L	R	L		
I1	MD	-	-	9.01	(6.37)	7.75	7.76	7.53	8.64	-	-	-	-
	BL	-	-	5.92	-	6.09	6.91	-	-	-	-	-	-
	CA	-	-	53.33	-	47.19	53.62	-	-	-	-	-	-
	CI	-	-	152.19	-	127.25	112.30	-	-	-	-	-	-
	CM	-	-	7.46	-	6.92	7.33	-	-	-	-	-	-
I2	MD	-	-	6.14	6.83	5.88	6.48	6.45	6.55	-	-	-	-
	BL	-	-	5.62	6.21	5.98	5.76	-	-	-	-	-	-
	CA	-	-	34.50	42.41	35.16	37.32	-	-	-	-	-	-
	CI	-	-	109.25	109.9	98.32	112.5	-	-	-	-	-	-
	CM	-	-	5.88	6.52	5.93	6.12	-	-	-	-	-	-
C	MD	-	-	7.53	8.06	6.53	7.32	7.02	6.65	-	-	7.74	-
	BL	-	-	6.92	7.90	7.84	7.72	-	-	-	-	8.37	-
	CA	-	-	52.10	63.67	51.19	56.51	-	-	-	-	64.78	-
	CI	-	-	108.81	102.02	83.29	94.81	-	-	-	-	92.47	-
	CM	-	-	7.22	7.98	7.185	7.52	-	-	-	-	8.05	-
Pm1	MD	-	-	7.72	7.70	(6.44)	6.86	6.86	-	-	-	-	-
	BL	-	-	9.98	9.68	9.68	9.49	-	-	-	-	-	-
	CA	-	-	77.04	74.53	62.33	65.10	-	-	-	-	-	-
	CI	-	-	77.35	79.54	66.52	72.28	-	-	-	-	-	-
	CM	-	-	8.85	8.69	8.06	8.17	-	-	-	-	-	-
Pm2	MD	-	-	6.70	6.80	6.80	(6.42)	-	-	-	-	-	-
	BL	-	-	9.11	7.68	9.80	10.13	-	-	-	-	-	-
	CA	-	-	61.037	52.22	66.64	65.03	-	-	-	-	-	-
	CI	-	-	73.54	88.54	69.38	63.37	-	-	-	-	-	-
	CM	-	-	7.90	7.24	8.3	8.275	-	-	-	-	-	-
M1	MD	-	-	10.54	10.83	(9.20)	(10.01)	-	-	-	-	(10.35)	-
	BL	-	-	-	8.91	11.72	11.92	-	-	-	-	-	-
	CA	-	-	-	96.49	107.82	119.31	-	-	-	-	-	-
	CI	-	-	-	121.54	78.49	83.97	-	-	-	-	-	-
	CM	-	-	-	9.87	10.46	10.96	-	-	-	-	-	-
M2	MD	-	-	-	9.56	-	(9.93)	-	-	-	-	8.70	9.23
	BL	-	-	-	9.38	-	(10.53)	-	-	-	-	11.85	11.84
	CA	-	-	-	89.67	-	104.56	-	-	-	-	103.09	109.28
	CI	-	-	-	101.91	-	94.30	-	-	-	-	73.41	77.95
	CM	-	-	-	9.47	-	10.23	-	-	-	-	10.27	10.53
M3	MD	-	8.33	-	-	8.93	-	-	-	-	8.13	-	-
	BL	-	10.14	-	-	10.75	-	-	-	-	9.79	-	-
	CA	-	84.46	-	-	95.99	-	-	-	-	79.59	-	-
	CI	-	82.14	-	-	83.06	-	-	-	-	83.04	-	-
		-	9.23	-	-	9.84	-	-	-	-	8.96	-	-

Table 5.10 continues: Odontometric data for Maxillary dentition

Tooth		Spe. 45		Spe. 47		Spe. 62		Spe. 65	
		R	L	R	L	R	L	R	L
I2	MD	6.59	-	-	-	-	-	-	-
	BL	4.98	-	-	-	-	-	-	-
	CA	32.81	-	-	-	-	-	-	-
	CI	132.32	-	-	-	-	-	-	-
	CM	5.78	-	-	-	-	-	-	-
C	MD	-	7.23	7.34	-	-	-	-	-
	BL	-	7.74	7.37	-	-	-	-	-
	CA	-	55.96	54.09	-	-	-	-	-
	CI	-	93.41	99.59	-	-	-	-	-
	CM	-	7.48	7.35	-	-	-	-	-
Pm1	MD	-	-	6.38	-	-	6.90	-	-
	BL	-	-	8.35	-	-	-	-	-
	CA	-	-	53.27	-	-	-	-	-
	CI	-	-	76.40	-	-	-	-	-
	CM	-	-	7.36	-	-	-	-	-
Pm2	MD	6.83	-	5.98	6.73	6.93	-	-	-
	BL	8.98	-	-	6.35	-	-	-	-
	CA	61.33	-	-	42.73	-	-	-	-
	CI	76.05	-	-	105.98	-	-	-	-
	CM	7.90	-	-	6.54	-	-	-	-
M1	MD	10.21	-	-	-	9.90	-	10.89	-
	BL	11.49	-	-	-	10.01	-	11.90	-
	CA	117.31	-	-	-	99.09	-	129.59	-
	CI	88.85	-	-	-	98.90	-	91.51	-
	CM	10.85	-	-	-	9.95	-	11.395	-
M2	MD	10.69	-	-	9.20	-	-	-	-
	BL	11.60	-	-	10.13	-	-	-	-
	CA	124	-	-	93.19	-	-	-	-
	CI	92.15	-	-	90.81	-	-	-	-
	CM	11.14	-	-	9.66	-	-	-	-

Table 5.11: Odontometric data for mandibular dentition

Tooth		Spe. 2		Spe. 6		Spe. 14		Spe. 18		Spe. 23	
		R	L	R	L	R	L	R	L	R	L
I1	MD	-	-	-	-	5.36	5.40	-	-	-	-
	BL	-	-	-	-	4.96	5.35	-	-	-	-
	CA	-	-	-	-	26.58	28.89	-	-	-	-
	CI	-	-	-	-	108.06	100.93	-	-	-	-
	CM	-	-	-	-	5.16	5.375	-	-	-	-
I2	MD	-	-	-	-	6.64	-	-	-	-	-
	BL	-	-	-	-	4.94	-	-	-	-	-
	CA	-	-	-	-	32.80	-	-	-	-	-
	CI	-	-	-	-	134.40	-	-	-	-	-
	CM	-	-	-	-	5.79	-	-	-	-	-
C	MD	-	-	-	-	-	6.68	-	-	-	6.00
	BL	-	-	-	-	-	6.19	-	-	-	7.21
	CA	-	-	-	-	-	41.34	-	-	-	43.26
	CI	-	-	-	-	-	107.91	-	-	-	83.21
	CM	-	-	-	-	-	6.435	-	-	-	6.60
Pm1	MD	5.98	5.97	-	-	-	7.34	-	-	-	5.90
	BL	7.14	7.17	-	-	-	6.16	-	-	-	6.82
	CA	42.69	42.80	-	-	-	45.21	-	-	-	40.23
	CI	83.75	83.26	-	-	-	119.15	-	-	-	86.51
	CM	6.56	6.57	-	-	-	6.75	-	-	-	6.36
Pm2	MD	6.99	6.09	-	-	-	6.18	6.97*	7.07*	-	6.40
	BL	8.08	7.59	-	-	-	6.36	8.47*	8.39*	-	7.29
	CA	56.47	46.22	-	-	-	39.30	59.03	59.31	-	46.65
	CI	86.50	80.23	-	-	-	97.16	82.29	84.26	-	87.79
	CM	7.53	6.84	-	-	-	6.27	7.72	7.73	-	6.84
M1	MD	9.68	-	-	-	11.73	10.27	-	-	11.09	9.29
	BL	9.86	-	-	-	10.80	9.32	-	-	-	10.58
	CA	95.44	-	-	-	126.68	95.71	-	-	-	98.28
	CI	98.17	-	-	-	108.61	110.19	-	-	-	87.80
	CM	9.77	-	-	-	11.265	9.795	-	-	-	9.93
M2	MD	9.96	-	-	-	-	10.91	(10.17)	-	10.63	9.92
	BL	10.03	-	-	-	-	9.42	9.59	-	10.08	-
	CA	99.89	-	-	-	-	102.77	97.53	-	107.15	-
	CI	99.30	-	-	-	-	115.81	106.04	-	105.45	-
	CM	9.99	-	-	-	-	10.165	9.88	-	10.35	-
M3	MD	-	-	-	(7.88)	9.60	9.60	-	-	-	-
	BL	-	-	-	-	9.06	9.90	-	-	-	-
	CA	-	-	-	-	86.97	95.04	-	-	-	-
	CI	-	-	-	-	105.96	96.96	-	-	-	-
	CM			-	-	9.33	9.75	-	-	-	-

*Indicates unidentified tooth

Table 5.11 continues: Odontometric data for mandibular dentition

Tooth		Spe. 41		Spe. 45		Spe. 47		Spe. 52		Spe. 65		Spe. 67	
		R	L	R	L	R	L	R	L	R	L	R	L
I1	MD	-	-	5.07	-	-	-	-	-	-	-	-	-
	BL	-	-	4.88	-	-	-	-	-	-	-	-	-
	CA	-	-	24.74	-	-	-	-	-	-	-	-	-
	CI	-	-	103.89	-	-	-	-	-	-	-	-	-
	CM	-	-	4.97	-	-	-	-	-	-	-	-	-
I2	MD	7.90	-	5.17	-	-	6.57	-	6.38	-	-	-	-
	BL	6.81	-	4.48	-	-	6.11	-	6.36	-	-	-	-
	CA	53.79	-	23.16	-	-	40.14	-	40.57	-	-	-	-
	CI	116	-	115.40	-	-	107.52	-	100.31	-	-	-	-
	CM	7.35	-	4.825	-	-	6.34	-	6.37	-	-	-	-
C	MD	-	-	6.66	-	-	-	-	-	-	-	-	-
	BL	-	-	5.55	-	-	-	-	-	-	-	-	-
	CA	-	-	36.96	-	-	-	-	-	-	-	-	-
	CI	-	-	120	-	-	-	-	-	-	-	-	-
	CM	-	-	6.10	-	-	-	-	-	-	-	-	-
Pm2	MD	-	-	7.01	-	-	-	-	-	-	-	-	-
	BL	-	-	7.09	-	-	-	-	-	-	-	-	-
	CA	-	-	49.70	-	-	-	-	-	-	-	-	-
	CI	-	-	98.87	-	-	-	-	-	-	-	-	-
	CM	-	-	7.05	-	-	-	-	-	-	-	-	-
M1	MD	-	-	10.87	-	-	-	-	-	-	9.62	-	-
	BL	-	-	10.17	-	-	-	-	-	-	9.50	-	-
	CA	-	-	110.54	-	-	-	-	-	-	91.39	-	-
	CI	-	-	106.88	-	-	-	-	-	-	101.26	-	-
	CM	-	-	10.52	-	-	-	-	-	-	9.56	-	-
M2	MD	-	-	9.47	-	-	-	-	-	-	9.42	-	-
	BL	-	-	9.13	-	-	-	-	-	-	9.54	-	-
	CA	-	-	86.46	-	-	-	-	-	-	89.86	-	-
	CI	-	-	103.72	-	-	-	-	-	-	98.74	-	-
	CM	-	-	9.3	-	-	-	-	-	-	9.48	-	-
M3	MD	-	-	-	-	-	-	-	-	-	-	10.16	(10.30)
	BL	-	-	-	-	-	-	-	-	-	-	9.84	(10.15)
	CA	-	-	-	-	-	-	-	-	-	-	99.97	104.54
	CI	-	-	-	-	-	-	-	-	-	-	103.25	101.47
	CM	-	-	-	-	-	-	-	-	-	-	10	10.22

6

Morphological and Pathological Observations

The section is divided into two parts. The first part discusses the morphological observations on Farmana skeletal material which includes crania, long bones, and dentition. The next section is about the pathological findings from the assemblage.

Cranial morphology

Cranial morphology is mainly based on shape and size which is calculated from cranial measurements. The morphology description is used for population comparisons. From Farmana three females (specimens 2, 18 and 20) and one male (specimen 67) provide a maximum number of morphological observations.

In Facial profile angle, out of 5 individuals, 3 are mesoprognathous (2 females and 1 male) and 2 are prognathous (1 female and 1 male).

In Nasal Profile Angle, out of 5 individuals, 3 are mesognathous (2 females and 1 male) and 2 are orthognathous (1 female and 1 male). In Alveolar profile angle, out of 5 individuals, 2 are hyperprognathous (1 female and 1 male), 2 prognathous (1 female and 1 male) and 1 orthognathous female. Out of 9 individuals in case of a cranial index, 2 females are ultradolichocranial, 2 (1 male and 1 female) hyperdolichocranial, 4 females are dolichocranial and 1 male is mesocranial. The Auriculo-vertical index is calculated for 9 individual, out of that, 8 are hypsicranial (5 females and 3 males) and 1 female is orthocranial. Out of 4 individuals, the length-height cranial index, vertical index, 1 male (66) is orthocranial and rest 3 females are chamaecranial having a low flat skull with a length-height index of less than 70.

In the Breadth-height cranial index, trans. Vertical index, out of 4 individuals, 2 females are acrocranial and 1 female and 1 male are metriocranial (acrocranial is being pyramidal or pointed at the top with a breadth-height index of 98 or above). All females (3 individuals) are eurymetopic when transverse fronto breadth index, the frontal index is calculated. The total facial index was calculated only for one female and indicated Leptoprosopic (long narrow face). Out of 3 individuals, 2 (1 female and 1 male) are hyperlepten and 1 female leption in Kollman`s upper facial index. Out of 9 individuals, 6 are hypsiconch (3 females, 2 males, and 1 adolesent) 3 females are mesoconch in orbital index. Out of 8 individuals, all 6 females are chamaerhine (broad nose) and out of 2 males, 1 is leptorhine (narrow nose) and 1 male hyperchamaerhine very broad nose. Mandibular index was calculated only for two females and both are Dolichostenomandibular. To conclude the cranial morphology, individual wise observations on indices are given in the following table to understand the general facial features (Table 6.1).

Table 6.1: Individual wise morphological features

Specimen no	Sex	Age	Index
2	F	50	Mesoprognathous, Orthognathous, Prognathous, Dolichocranial, Hypsicranial, Hypsiconch, Chamaerhine, Dolichostenomandibular
18	F	40-45	Prognathous, Mesognathous, Hyperprognathous, Hyperdolichocranial, Hypsicranial, Chamaecranial, Acrocranial, Eurymetopic, Hyperlepten, Hypsiconch, Chamaerhine
20	F	35-40	Mesoprognathous, Mesognathous, Orthognathous, Dolichocranial, Hypsicranial, Eurymetopic, Leptoprosopic, Lepton, Mesoconch, Chamaerhine, Dolichostenomandibular
26	F	40-45	Dolichocranial, Orthocranial, Chamaecranial, Metriocrania, Hypsiconch
23	F	18-20	Mesoconch, Chamaerhine
26	F	40-45	Chamaerhine
32	F	18-19	Dolichocranial, Hypsicranial
53	F	30	Ultradolichocranial, Mesoconch
62	F	15	Ultradolichocranial, Hypsicranial, Chamaecranial, Acrocranial, Eurymetopic, Chamaerhine
14	M	20-25	Prognathous, Mesognathous, Hyperprognathous, Hyperdolichocranial, Hypsicranial, Leptorhine
66	M	50	Mesocranial, Hypsicranial, Orthocranial, Metriocranial, Hypsiconch
67	M	35	Mesoprognathous, Orthognathous, Prognathous, Hypsicranial, Hyperlepten, Hypsiconch, hyperchamaerhine

Many of the traits are mixed in both the sexes. There are few indices which have female dominance. In the cranial index, females, head tend to be Ultradolichocranial and dolichocranial which indicates long head. In ariculo-vertical index all females are hypsicranial. In length height vertical index females are chamaecranial. In frontal index all 3 females are erymetopic, male indices are not available for comparison. In nasal index, all 6 females come under the broad nose and in 2 males one is with a narrow nose and one with the very broad nose. It is difficult to say that female belongs to one type of facial features. In case of a male, the sample size is very small to come to any form of conclusion.

Post cranial morphology

There are hardly complete preserved post-cranial bones from Farmana. Therefore, limited observations were conducted. The right side femoral lesser tronchanter of skeleton 1 is strongly developed and laterally placed (Fig. 6.1). The same case is also seen on the left femur of skeleton 10 (Fig. 6.2). It is very difficult to

Figure 6.1: Burial 1, strongly developed and laterally placed lesser trochanter on the right femur

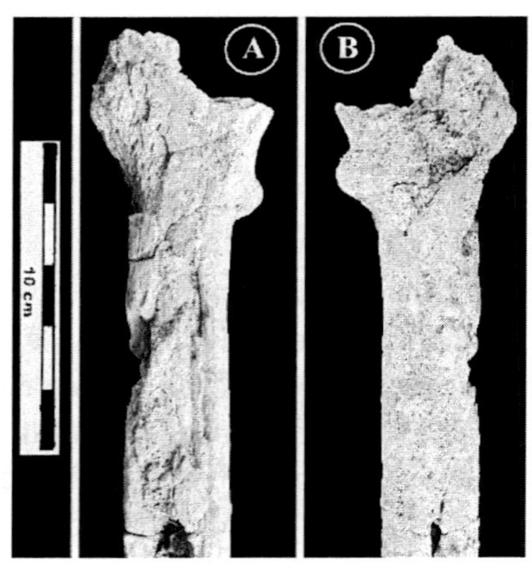

Figure 6.2: Burial 10, strongly developed and laterally placed lesser trochanter on the left femur

say much on the prominent lesser tronchanter. It is possible that the excessive physical activity may have led to the stronger muscle attachment area. The other sides of bone in both cases not preserved and therefore, it is difficult to see whether the development was bilaterally present or is only on one side of the body.

Dental morphology

There are certain dental traits prominently seen in a particular population and a tool for population comparison in past and present. In Farmana, Other than molar morphological observation only one dental trait was observed (Table 6.2, 6.3 and 6.4). (see next page)

Out of 21 observed incisors, only 4 incisors showed shoveling (19%). Individual 14 has shoveling of grade 2 on Maxillary LI2. Individual 41 also has grade 2 shoveling on mandibular RI2 on the lingual side. Mandibular LI2 of Individual 47 shows grade 4 shoveling on the lingual side.

Pathological observations

Palaeopathology essentially can be defined as the study of (logos) ancient (palaeo) suffering (pathos) in both humans and other animals. It is a discipline that aims to trace the origin, evolution, and history of disease over long periods of time through pathological changes which represent diseases suffered in life and observed in human remains buried at archaeological sites. This evidence of both acute injuries and chronic illnesses tells us a great deal about how individuals and populations experienced various challenges to their health. For the interpretation, diagnosis, and influence of diseases, variables such as individual's living environment, diet, work (occupation), conflict, and the ancient means of curing and mending have to considerate (Roberts 2009). Palaeopathologists have the benefit of being able to study the remains of the diseased directly, although usually only in a fraction, and this ability may be the only factor in their favor. The principal disadvantage that constrains palaeopathologists is that their study is restricted largely to those diseases that affect the skeleton. Thus, it is generally impossible or rare chances for palaeopathologists to determine the cause of death of those they examine (Waldorn 2008). Determining the cause of the death is often a speculation (Roberts and Manchester 1995). The other major problem is that there is no agreed system for diagnosing disease in the skeleton to which all (or even the majority of) palaeopathologists subscribe, thus rendering comparisons between different studies somewhat arbitrary at best, and invalid at worst (Waldorn 2008). The population studied are dead and may not represent the complete population and sample representativity is difficult to assess (Roberts and Manchester 1995).

Very few pathologies are observed on the Farmana skeletal assemblage. The partial preservation of bones limits the proper and complete understanding of lesions. Noted diseases include trauma, nutritional deficiency some old age related joint problems on bones and on teeth, other than attrition, caries and probable case of dental fluorosis has been identified.

Trauma

Trauma in palaeopathological literature is defined as any bodily injury. It is divided into categories including fractures, crushing injuries, sharp force wounds, dislocations, deformation, scalping, mutilation, trepanation, traumatic problems arising from pregnancy (*symphysis pubica*), soft-tissue trauma, osteochondritis dissecans (fragmentation and disruption of articular cartilage consequent upon trauma) etc. (Bennike 2008). Trauma may be defined many ways but conventionally is understood to refer to an injury to living tissue that is caused by a force or mechanism extrinsic to the body. The anatomical importance and sociocultural implications of trauma in antiquity long have been recognized and the description of trauma in human skeletal remains and the identification and comparison of trauma patterns among ancient populations, therefore, have a lengthy history (Lovell 1997).

Table 6.2: Morphological observations on adult Maxillary dentition

Traits	Side	Individual																	
Maxilla		Burial no: 1			Burial no: 14			Burial no: 18			Burial no: 20			Burial no: 26			Burial no: 65		
		Age: 18-20			Age:20-25 years			Age:40-45			Age: 35-40			Age:40-45			Age:Around 30		
		Sex: Male			Sex: Male			Sex: Female			Sex: Female			Sex: Female			Sex: Female?		
		M1	M2	M1	M1	M3	M3	M1	M2	M3	M1	M2	M3	M1	M2	M3	M1	M2	M3
Hypocone	R	-	-	-	5	-	0	-	?	-	3.5?	-	0?	-	?	0	3	-	-
	L	1	-	-	5	5	-	-	-	-	-	-	-	-	-	0	-	-	-
Metacone	R	-	-	-	5	-	3.5	-	4	-	4	-	3	-	4	3	?	-	-
	L	3	-	-	5	4	-	-	-	-	-	-	-	-	-	3	-	-	-
Metaconule	R	-	-	-	0	-	0	-	?	-	?	-	?	-	-	-	?	-	-
	L	0	-	-	0	0	-	-	-	-	-	-	-	-	-	-	-	-	-
Carabelli's cusp	R	-	-	-	-	-	6	-	-	-	-	-	-	-	-	-		-	-
	L	-	-	-	-	-	-	-	-	-	-	-	-	-	-	-		-	-

Table 6.3: Morphological observations on sub-adult Maxillary dentition

Traits	Side	Individual																	
		Burial no: 5			Burial no: 15			Burial no: 41			Burial no: 45			Burial no: 52			Burial no: 62		
		Age: 3.5-4 years			Age:2 years			Age:7-8			Age: 13-15			Age: 3.5 years			Age: 15		
		Sex: NA			Sex: NA			Sex: NA			Sex: NA			Sex: NA			Sex: Female?		
		dm2	M1	M2	dm2	M1	M2	dm2	M1	M2	M1	M2	M3	dm2	M1	M2	M1	M2	M3
Hypocone	R	3.5	-	-	-	3.5	-	-	3	0	3.5	1	-	4	-	-	3	-	-
	L	-	-	-	-	5	-	-	-	0	-	-	-	3.5	-	-	-	-	-
Metacone	R	4	-	-	-	4	-	-	4	2	4	3.5	-	4	-	-	4	-	-
	L	-	-	-	-	4	-	-	-	3.5	-	-	-	3.5	-	-		-	-
Metaconule	R	0	-	-	-	2	-	-	-	-	-	-	-	2	-	-	0	-	-
	L	-	-	-	-	2	-	-	-	-	-	-	-	2	-	-	-	-	-
Carabelli's cusp	R	-	-	-	-	-	-	-	-	-	-	-	-	-	-	-	-	-	-
	L	-	-	-	-	-	-	-	-	-	-	-	-	-	-	-	-	-	-

Table 6.4: Morphological observations on mandibular dentition

Traits	Side	Individual																				
		Burial no: 14			Burial no 23			Burial no: 45			Burial no: 54			Burial no: 58			Burial no: 65			Burial no: 67		
		Age: 20-25			Age: 18-20			Age: 13-15			Age: 30-35			Age: Around 20			Age: 30			Age: 35		
		Sex: Male			Sex: Female			Sex: NA			Sex: Male?			Sex: ?			Sex: Female?			Sex: Male		
		M1	M2	M3	M1	M2	M3	M1	M2	M3	M1	M2	M3	M1	M2	M3	M1	M2	M3	M1	M2	M3
Groove pattern	R	Y?	-	-	-	+?	+	Y?	+	-	+?	-	-	-	+	-		-	-			
	L	Y?	+?	-	×	+	-	-	-	-	-	-	-	-		-	?	-	-			
Cusp Number	R	5	-	4	4	4?	4	5	4	-	4	-	-	-	4	-		-	-			4?
	L	5	4	4	4	4	-		-	-	-	-	-	-		-	4	-	-			

Farmana Burial 39b gives evidence of unhealed cranial trauma (Fig. 6.3, 6.4 and 6.5) on the anterior portion of left parietal. On the left side near coronal suture, there is a evidence of trauma, in the healing process. The trauma is visible as a hole with rounded edges. At the same time near a periphery, there is a cracking pattern seen as radiating circular lines and a depression in the middle area. This is the typical trauma occurred by a blunt object. The affected area is 5 x 5 cm. The bone is thin in the middle, where the secondary bone is forming. There is an evidence of some blunt force trauma with low velocity and is identified as depression fracture. In the case of a "depression" fracture involving the cranial vault, the outer cortex of the bone is clearly depressed inward while the underlying diploe is "compressed." If the inner cortex is also involved, and the compressed diploe will also be "depressed." Referring to such fractures as "depressed" rather than "compressed" often becomes a matter of convention rather than the accurate description (Merbs 1989). It is notable that the trauma is not the immediate cause of death. The person was alive probably for a month after the injury and eventually died due to secondary bone infection.

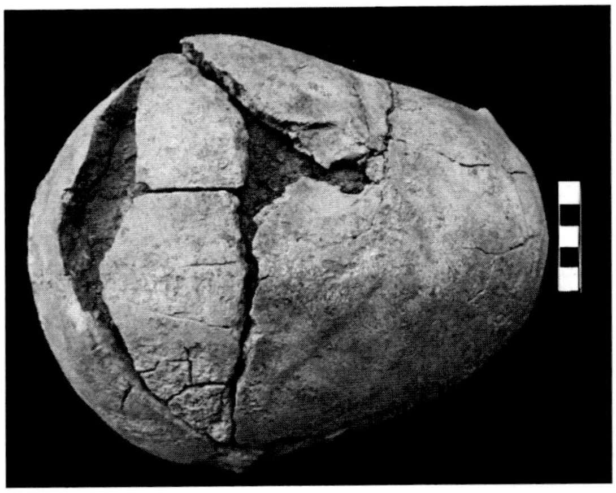

Figure 6.3: Burial 39b, evidence of unhealed cranial trauma

Figure 6.4: Burial 39b, close up of the trauma

Figure 6.5: Burial 39b, inner table of trauma

This is a peculiar burial. There were two crania buried in the pit with 12 pots towards the north. This is a very large pit and the skulls and the pottery being placed on the northen area of the burial. The skull 39b was from found upside down position without basal region. The other skull was slightly above and found resting on the basal region. The trauma and the burial condition of this specimen is different from the other burials. The reason behind this unusal burial practice is difficult to understand.

Metabolic bone disease

Metabolic bone disease can be defined as disease-causing disruption of normal bone formation, remodelling or mineralization, or a combination of these (Albright and Riefenstein, 1948). There are few conditions which can come under this category, namely vitamin D deficiency disease (rickets, osteomalacia), vitamin C deficiency disease (scurvy), enamel hypoplasia, Harris lines, osteoporosis and Paget's disease of bone, etc. The first four conditions are indicators of past lifeways and diet and nutrition, hence, form important tools in biocultural studies of past populations (Mays 2008). Vitamin D deficiency disease is intimately related to aspects of culture and lifestyle which affect the exposure of skin to natural light, enamel hypoplasia and Harris line indicators of nutritional deficiencies of early/growing ages. Scurvy is an indicator of dietary imbalance or poor food preparation techniques. Osteoporosis and Paget's disease demonstrate the potential of palaeopathology to contribute to our understanding of currently important diseases.

From Farmana there is evidence of iron deficiency anemia observed on burial 26, burial 53 and burial 66. Burial 26 has evidence of porosity on the frontal bone as well as have a very thick occipital bone. This individual is a female aged around 40 - 45 years old (Fig. 6.6 and 6.7). The individual 53 has porosity on the frontal bone and also shows bone thickening. This kind of thick cranial bones is seen for burial 66 also. The individual 53 is a middle-aged (around 30 y) woman and the 66 individual is old (50+) male person. Although it is difficult to interpret the anomalies one can see the probability of health deterioration in old age as well as the in case of women.

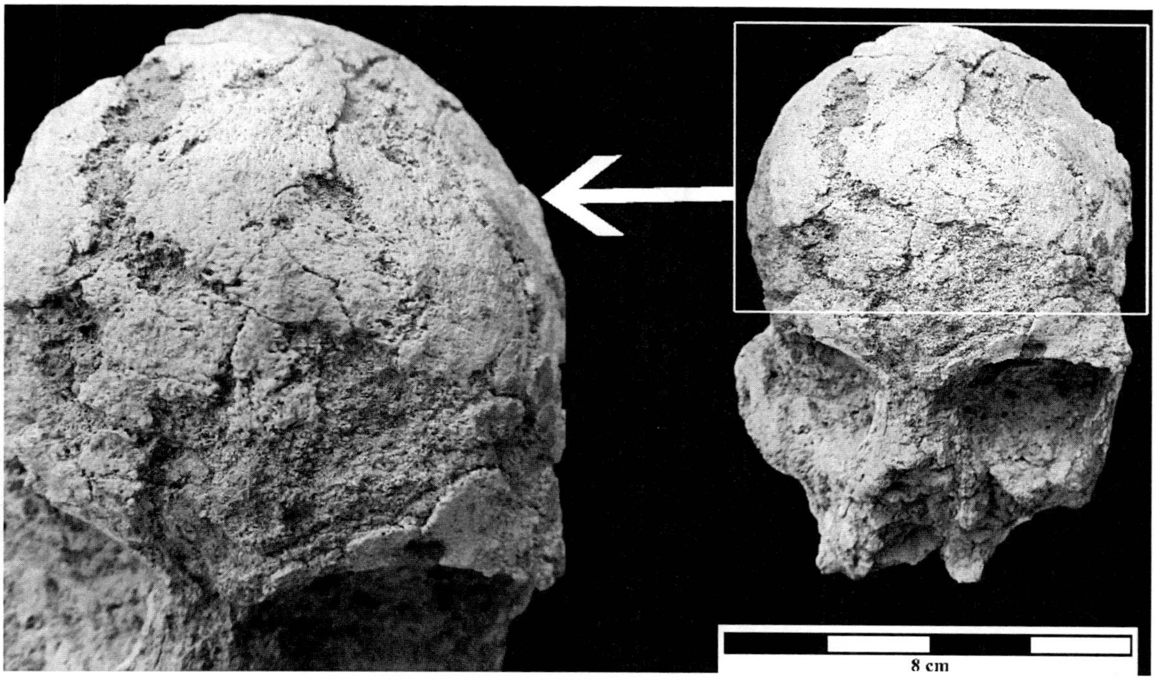

Figure 6.6: Burial 26, porosity on frontal bone

Figure 6.7: Burial 26, thick occipital bone

Osteoarthritis

It is most commonly found disease from archaeological specimens. It is non-inflammatory disease and involves all the synovial joints. Typical features of osteoarthritis (degenerative joint disease) including lipping (bony spur or osteophytic development) marginal to the articular surface, porosity of the surface and eburnation.

Three major components of skeletal involvement is seen in the pathology of osteoarthritis:

1. breakdown of articular cartilage, which may result in bone on bone contact and abnormal abrasion of the subchondral bone,
2. reactive bone formation (sclerosis) both in the subchondral compact bone (eburnation) and in the trabeculae underlying the affected subchondral compact bone and possibly associated with cyst formation, and
3. new growth of cartilage and bone at the joint margins (osteophytes). Inflammation does occur in some destructive manifestations of osteoarthritis (Cooper 1998; Dieppe and Lim 1998; Solomon 2001), but relatively uncommon.

These bone changes are slow but progressive and demonstrate by alterations of the articular cartilage. There are two types of osteoarthritis, primary osteoarthritis tends to occur in later life as a result of multiple factors, including biomechanical stress, trauma, etcetera and secondary osteoarthritis develops earlier in life in joints that are abnormal because of other pathological conditions, such as slipped femoral epiphysis and Legge-Perthes disease or metabolic problems such as ochronosis. Arthritis of a single joint is known as monoarticular. This type tends to be associated with the secondary osteoarthritis of the younger age range. The most common type of osteoarthritis is polyarticular, in which many joints are involved. The usual form of this type is for the joints of the hands to be involved along with at least some other joints, typically the knees or spine (Dieppe and Lim 1998).

For burial 64 the angle of the right femoral neck is changed (Fig. 6.8). The left side femur does not have articulated proximal side to know the exact orientation of neck region. At the same time lipping is seen on

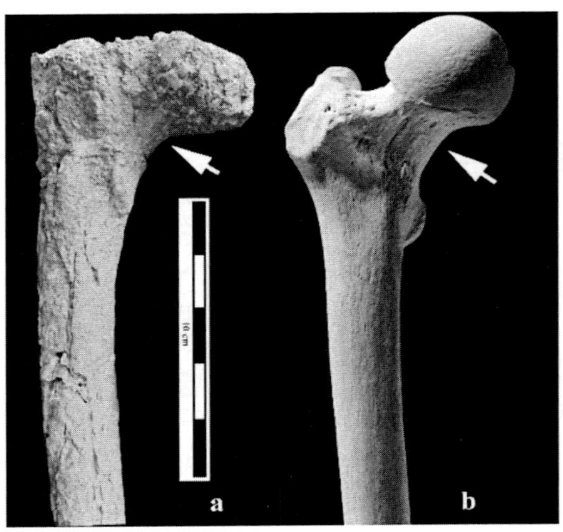

Figure 6.8: Burial 64, a. changed angle of right femoral neck, b. normal femoral neck

the 3rd, 4th and 5th lumber vertebrae (Fig. 6.9). This is a young male aged around 20 to 25 year. Generally, the presence of vertebral lipping is related to old age but the presence of lipping on this individual may indicate the stress on the body due to labours work. Another individual, burial 67 gives evidence of lipping on 4th and 5th lumber vertebrae (Fig. 6.10). This male individual is middle aged around 35 years old. This also suggests the physical stress on the lower back.

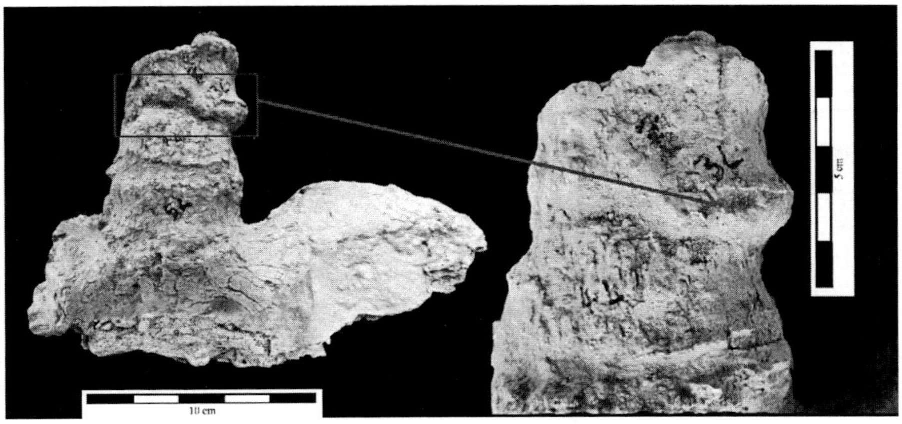

Figure 6.9: Burial 64, lipping seen on the 3rd, 4th and 5th lumber vertebrae

Figure 6.10: Burial 67, a. lipping on 4th and 5th lumber vertebrae, b. close up of the lipping

Dental Wear

Attrition or wear on teeth is a mechanical process and happens when teeth are used for mastication. There are two main types of wear- natural mastication (physiologic attrition) and attrition, often localized, caused by abnormal use or position of teeth (pathologic attrition). The factors contributing to attrition are varied and include the occlusion of the opposing teeth and the quality of the teeth (Pindborg 1970). The process of tooth wear begins with enamel loss and is followed by secondary dentin deposition. Tooth wear may have resulted from a variety of processes, including attrition, abrasion, and erosion.

Other than the minimum to moderate amount of wear has been observed on the Farmana dentition which is mentioned in the tabular form (Table 6.5). In the present assembledge there are older females and they show heavy wear pattern. For example, burial 2 shows heavy attrition where only enamel ring is present. This female is above 50 years old (Fig. 6.11). For individual from burial 6 has heavy dental wear resulting into the complete removal of the right side premolars crown. It seems that the anterior teeth of this female who was around 40 to 45 years old were completely worn out (Fig. 6.12). There are no other anterior teeth present in the collection to confirm this statement. Burial 18 belongs to female aged around 40 to years old shows heavy attrition on maxillary posterior teeth (Fig. 6.13).

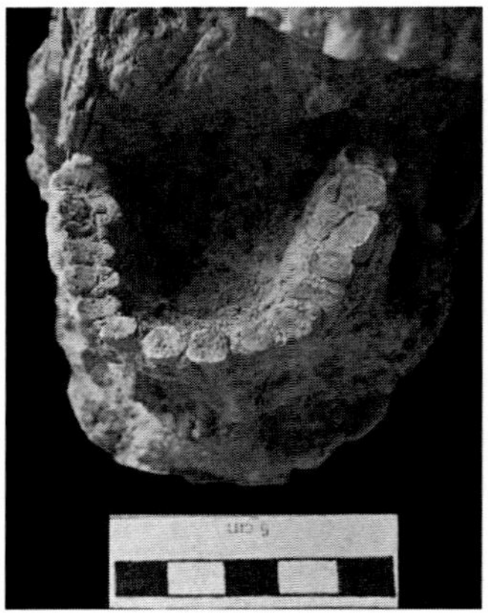

Figure 6.11: Burial 2, heavy attrition on mandibular teeth

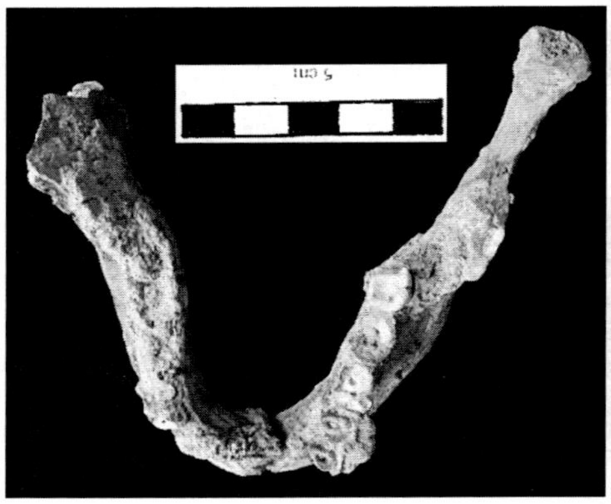

Figure 6.12: Burial 6, heavy attrition on mandibular teeth

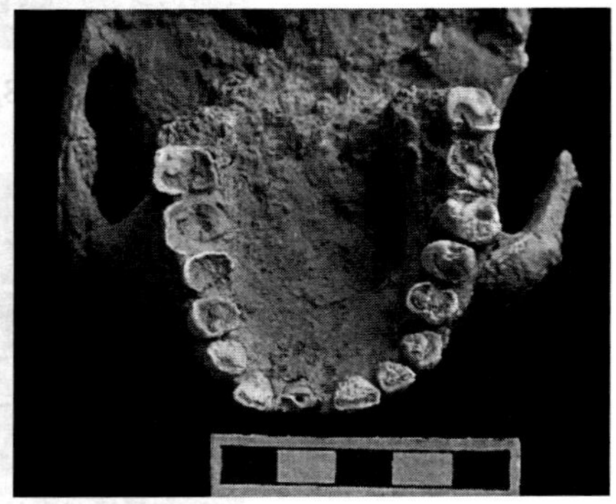

Figure 6.13: Burial 18, heavy wear on maxillary teeth

Caries

Caries is a progressive demineralization of the tooth caused by localized fermentation of food sugars by dental plaque (Mandel, 1979). Caries is considered an infectious disease because bacterial organisms become concentrated on specific tooth sites in the form of an adherent gelatinous mat known as bacterial plaque. The presence of sucrose in association with acidogenic bacteria produces demineralization of enamel and dentine resulting in cavitation (Luckas 1989). Carries are frequently seen on the molars and premolars than the anterior teeth like incisors and canines. It is also observed that mandibular teeth are affected more than the maxillary teeth. Similarly, it is noted that caries and dental ware, abrasion and chipping have a complex relationship which adds yet another range of factors to the changing pattern of caries with increasing age (Hillson 2001). Untreated caries may result in destruction of the entire crown and/or significant portions of the root. Exposure of the pulp chamber creates a high risk of infection with the almost inevitable sequelae of abscess and destruction of the supporting alveolar bone and process (Ortner 2003). The carbohydrate based diet with refined sugar and flour along with increased adhesiveness of some foods, caries frequency has become greater with the time from introduction of agriculture till recent times.

Individual from burial 18 have caries infection on maxillary LM1 and RM3 and on mandibular RM2. The maxillary RM3 probably had caries on the Mesio-Lingual side (Fig. 6.14). The M2 crown from the same side is missing. LM1 has lost its crown from lingual side probably due to caries and only the buccal wall remains. For mandibular right second molar, distal half of crown is damaged (Fig. 6.15). Both maxillary and mandibular teeth shown extensive wear pattern on the left side. Maxillary teeth indicate extensive use of left side for the masticatory purpose. The wear pattern on the mandibular teeth cannot be measured due to post-mortem damage. This individual is old age female, therefore, extensive wear and caries infection can be related to old age.

Figure 6.14: Burial 18, probable caries on maxillary RM3 on Mesio-Lingual side

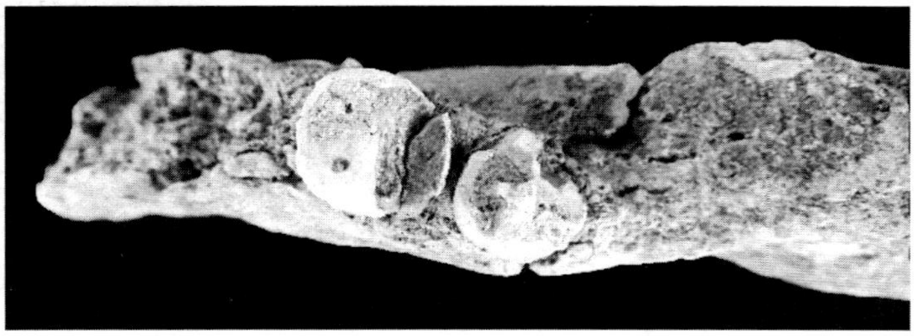

Figure 6.15: Burial 18, caries on mandibular RM2

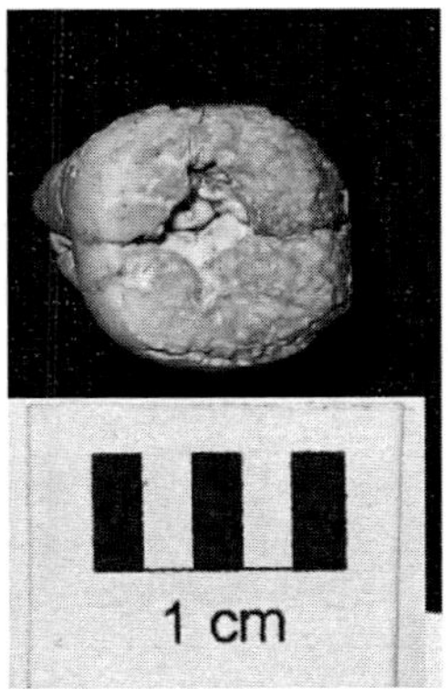

Figure 6.16: Burial 54, caries infection on the occlusal surface of mandibular RM1

Burial no 54 has caries infection on the occlusal surface of first right mandibular molar (Fig. 6.16). Burial no 65 (see figure 4.14) shows the beginning of caries is seen on a mandibular first left mandibular molar. The diameter of the infection is around 5mm. Both individuals are males in their late twenties (25 to 30 years). Presence of dental caries at young age probably indicate the dietary origin coupled with oral unhygienic practices behind the infection.

Enamel Hypoplasia

During development, teeth require adequate nutritional input, including protein, calcium, phosphate, trace elements, and vitamins A, C, and D. Inadequacies in these components may result in grossly abnormal teeth or in teeth more susceptible to wear and microbial invasion (caries). Various components, such as the enamel or dentin, may be differently affected by morbid conditions that occur after dental development is complete. Enamel hypoplasias, including linear and localized enamel hypoplasias (mainly on deciduous teeth), are a well-known feature in archaeological human skeletal remains that provide an indicator of some type of physiological stress associated with the formation of the affected enamel during the development of the tooth. Bouts of malnutrition, disease, and fever are known to depress the activity of the ameloblasts and to result in the production of a thin and poorly calcified enamel matrix, with the formation of linearly distributed pits or grooves of defective enamel (Ortener and Putschar 2003).

From this site, only two cases are identified, one is a two year old child (Burial 15) and another young female aged between 18-25 years. In case of a child, enamel pitting is seen on one side of the maxillary left first molar on mesio-lingual cusp and surface is very disturbed (Fig. 6.17) and the normal enamel layer can be seen on the mesio-buccal side. The tooth is still forming. This indicates probably the child was suffering from prolonged health issues and eventually succumbed to it.

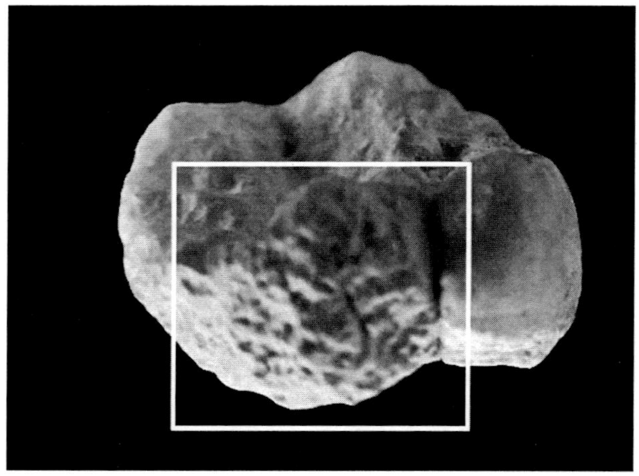

Figure 6.17: Burial 15, disturbed enamel on maxillary LM1

A case of linear enamel hypoplasia is observed on the maxillary RI1, RC and RPm1 of burial no 23 (Fig. 6.18). The lines are not very visible but traces can be seen. On right first incisor the line is in the middle of the crown. The incisor crown calcification starts at the age of 3 to 4 months and completes around 4 to 5 years. If the line is in the middle of the crown, then the individual had some physiological stress around 2 to 2.5 years. In case of canine, the crown calcification starts from 4 to 5 months and complete around 6 to 7 years. The line occurs after the 3/4th of the crown was formed. So probably another stress episode was around 4 years of age. In case of the first premolar, the crown calcification starts around 18 to 24 months and complete around 5 to 6 years. The line occurs when half-crown was formed when the child was around 4 years old. This shows this female suffered physiological stress at least two times in her childhood, one around 2.5 years and another around 4. The calculation is done using the criteria of crown formation timing to the crown completion and measuring the line from cemento-enamel junction (Mushrif-Tirpathy and Walimbe 2006).

Figure 6.18: Burial 23, linear enamel hypoplasia on the maxillary RI1, RC and RPm1

Table 6.5: Grade of Attrition on Farmana dentition

No.	Age	Sex	Maxilla																Mandible															
			I1		I2		C		Pm1		Pm2		M1		M2		M3		I1		I2		C		Pm1		Pm2		M1		M2		M3	
			R	L	R	L	R	L	R	L	R	L	R	L	R	L	R	L	R	L	R	L	R	L	R	L	R	L	R	L	R	L	R	L
1	18-20	Male	-	-	-	-	-	-	-	-	-	-	-	-	-	-	-	0	-	-	-	-	-	-	-	-	-	-	-	-	-	-	-	-
2	50+	Female	7	8	6	6	6	6	6	6	6	6	9	9	8	8	9	9	7	7	8	8	8	7	8	7	8	7	9	-	9	9	8	8
6	40-45	Female	-	-	-	-	-	-	-	-	-	-	-	-	-	-	-	-	-	-	-	-	-	-	-	-	-	-	-	5	-	-	-	5
11	45±5	Female	-	-	-	-	-	-	-	-	-	-	-	-	-	-	-	-	-	-	-	-	-	-	-	-	-	-	-	-	-	8	-	8
14	25	Male	3		2	2	3	3	2	2	2	2	-	5	-	4	-	-	3	3	3	-	-	2	-	1	-	2	5	5	-	3	1	1
18	40-45	Female	6	6	6	6	6	6	6	6	5	7	4	9	5	8	-	6	-	-	-	-	-	-	-	-	6	6	-	-	6	-	-	-
20	35-40	Female	-	-	-	-	-	-	-	-	-	-	7	-	-	-	4	-	-	-	-	-	-	-	-	-	-	-	-	-	-	-	-	-
23	18-20	Female	-	-	-	-	-	-	-	-	-	-	-	-	-	-	-	-	-	-	-	-	-	-	-	-	-	-	0	0	0	0	0	-
26	40-45	Female	-	-	-	-	-	-	-	-	7	-	-	-	6	-	6	6	-	-	-	-	-	-	-	-	-	-	-	-	-	-	-	-
41	7-8	-	-	-	-	-	-	-	-	-	-	-	0	-	-	-	-	-	-	-	-	-	-	-	-	-	-	-	-	-	-	-	-	-
45	13-15	-	-	-	0	-	2	-	0	-	1	-	4	-	2	-	-	-	3	-	2	-	3	-	-	-	1	-	5	-	1	-	-	-
54	30	Male	-	-	-	-	-	-	-	-		-		-	-	-	-	-	-	-	-	-	-	-	-	-	-	-	6		-	-	-	-
62	15	Female	-	-	-	-	-	-	-	-	2	-	5	-	-	-	-	-	-	-	-	-	-	-	-	-	-	-	-	-	-	-	-	-
65	50	Male	-	-	-	-	-	-	-	-	-	-	-	-	-	-	-	-	-	-	-	-	-	-	3	-	-	-	7	7	-	6	-	-
67	35	Male	-	-	-	-	-	-	-	-	-	-	-	-	-	-	-	-	-	-	-	-	-	7	-	-	-	-	-	-	-	-	6	7

Dental fluorosis

Dental fluorosis otherwise known as mottled teeth, brown stain or discolouration of enamel has been noticed by many scholars since 1880s. Dental fluorosis results in porosity of the surface and subsurface enamel by which enamel appears opaque. In the clinical features changes display fine white opaque lines running across the tooth on all parts of the enamel to entirely chalky white teeth. In other cases, the enamel may be so porous (or hypomineralized) that the outer enamel breaks apart post-eruptively and the exposed porous subsurface enamel becomes discoloured (Fejerskov *et. al.* 1990). The first index to grade dental fluorosis was developed by Dean in 1934 which is known as Dean's index (Dean 1934). Later he modified the observations in 1942 (Dean 1942). Abnormalities, including formation of brown spots in dental enamel and skeletal fluorosis begin to occur at concentrations of 2 ppm while more serious problems are associated with greater concentrations (Resnick 1995: 3321). Prolonged intake of high levels of fluorine can affect the structure and appearance of bone and teeth (Johnson 1965). Fluorine substitutes for the hydroxyl ion in the hydroxyapatite crystal of mineralized tissues to create fluorapatite, which is a more stable crystal structure. In addition to the formation of fluorapatite, fluorine at toxic levels in the serum stimulates osteoblast activity (Resnick 1995: 3324), which may explain abnormal bone formation seen in severe cases of fluorosis. Bone changes are observed only in long-standing and severe cases (Flemming *et al.* 1932, Sankaran and Gadekar 1964). Abnormal bone may form on any surface, but is particularly apparent in association with the insertions of tendons and ligaments where irregular bony excrescences form. From Farmana the evidence of fluorosis is found only on three individual. From burial 15, enamel pitting is seen on half calcified crown of maxillary molar around 2 year child which is related to enamel hypoplasia as well as the beginning of the dental fluorosis.

For burial no 14 mandibular first LPm2 shows little brownish pink colour tinge on the enamel indicating dental fluorosis. This is a 25 years male individual. For burial no 45 maxillary RI1, RI2, RPm2, RM1 and mandibular RC and LC show a brownish pink colour tinge on the enamel, indicating dental fluorosis. This is an adolescent individual belonging to 13-15 years of age bracket.

As seen, it is very difficult to say overall health of the population. But at large we can understand that the Farmana population seems to be healthy. Age-related bone changes and few bone modifications probably related to stress on particular bone or part of the body is visible. In dental pathologies including caries are found coupled with extreme wear seen on old individuals. Nutritional insults in form of enamel hypoplasia and porosity on crania is indicating the population may have suffered from the nutritional deficiencies.

7

Concluions

The Harappan phase from the Indian sub-continent represented by large number of human skeletons but they are mainly from the Harappa. There are other sites like Mohenjo Daro, Rupar, Kalibangan, Lothal, Dholavira and late Harappan site Sinauli which has provided human skeletons but they are very few in numbers. Some of them are partially studied or unstudied (Mushrif-Tripathy *et.al* 2016). As Kenoyer and Meadows (2016) summarised findings from the remains, a maximum number of human remains do not go beyond 50 individuals which is very less in comparison with Harappa where they have excavated 280 burials. Even in Farmana, though there are 70 burial pits recorded, only 35 individuals were excavated from the cemetery.

Human skeletal remains from Harappan context are always used for racial classifications, various 'types' of populations and mixing or merging of cultures. In archaeological context, 'racial' similarities or differences in two skeletal populations were used to emphasize either cultural contact or changes in the material culture. This was the trend of the early 20th century when theories of invasion, migration and 'mixing of blood' were the answers to diversities or 'discrepancies' noted in the skeletal record. In other words, anthropological research was guided by archaeological needs and the anthropological evidence was used primarily to complement archaeological hypotheses of cultural migration or diffusion. From these skeletal series, Harappa and Mohenjo-daro have been rigorously examined for craniometric variables (Guha B.S. and P.C. Basu. 1938, MacKay E.J.H. 1938, Marshall J. 1931). Their studies were mainly based on the racial classifications of skeletal populations. On the basis of certain cranial measurements, it was being shown that despite the skeletal material coming from three different deposits at Harappa, the skeletons belong to a single morphologically homogeneous series. Assessment of a biological continuum and affinities of the Pre-Harappan and Harappan population have always been a matter of prime interest to archaeologists as well as skeletal biologists (Kennedy K.A.R. 1982, Kennedy K.A.R. 1984a). Kennedy discussed Mohenjodaro assemblage showing more dolichocranial or long headedness in comparison with brachycranial or broad headedness which was considered as a deviation from the Mediterranean features by most of the anthropologist working on the material (Kennedy 2003).

Harappan skeletal remains are also in focused to describe the mythical massacre of the people commonly described as 'Aryan invasion'. The proof of so-called invasion is based on the few scattered skeletal remains from Mohenjodaro. It was suggested on the base of "a group of jumbled up skeletons (Khan 1968: 61)", that they were the victim of the epidemic, a sacrifice (Keith 1931), a natural disaster or slaughter by armed attack. Wheeler (1968) stretched this evidence to the massacre victims and said that these are the last defender of Mohenjodaro against attacking Aryans whose invasion led to the decline of the civilization.

There were a lot of argument and counter arguments to prove or to disprove the Aryan invasion since 1964 (Dales 1964). There was the very strong opposition of the Aryan 'race' among foreign scholars and Indian scholars (mentioned in Danino 2016 (page 206). After restudying the skeletal material from

Mohenjodaro Kennedy (1995) came to the conclusion that there is not much evidence to prove the foreign element in Harappa. Kennedy (1995: 54) mentions that "our multivariate approach does not define the biological identity of an ancient Aryan population, but it does indicate that the Indus Valley and Gandhara peoples shared a number of craniometric, odontometric and discrete traits that point to a high degree of biological affinity", thus completely denying the theory of 'Aryan invasion' (Kennedy K.A.R. 1984b, Kennedy K.A.R. 1995, Walimbe S.R. 1993, Walimbe 2014).

A study based on cranial non-metric morphological traits Hemphill *et al.* (1991) suggests that there existed two phases of biological discontinuity within the Indus valley from the Neolithic times to the Christian era. The first is said to occur between 6000 and 4500 B.C. which is reflected in the strong differences irrespective of the occupational continuity between the Neolithic and Chalcolithic inhabitants of Mehrgarh. The second discontinuity exists between the inhabitants of Harappa, Chalcolithic Mehrgarh, and post-Harappan Timargarha on the one hand, and the Early Iron Age (better known as the Gandhara Grave culture) inhabitants of Sarai Khola, on the other, between 800 and 200 B.C.

The skeletal series unearthed from Farmana is important in this regard. Although the preservation of 35 individuals from the cemetery is far from satisfactory, these remains have provided some clues about the bygone population. It is also interesting to notice that not all were given burials. Very few selected people were buried in the cemetery. It shows that there were many ways for disposing of the dead. There are few secondary and symbolic burials indicates, even though there are some common practices observed, every individual was buried with a slight variation. There are 24 primary burials and in that nine belongs to males, 12 females and five children and there are ten secondary burials out of that, three of males, two of females and four of children below 8 years (Table 7.1). It is evident that in Farmana cemetery, only some part of the population represented. As seen in the following table only ten individuals represents period II B and eighteen from period IIC in the span of 400 years.

Table 7.1: Composition of the cemetery in Farmana

Period	Primary burial (Spe. No)			Secondary burial (Spe. No)			Total
	Male	Female	Child	Male	Female	Child	
Burials from 2007-08 excavation	1	2, 6	3*, 5	-	-	-	5
Period IIA 2600 – 2400 BCE	-	32	28	-	-	-	2
Period IIB 2400 – 2200 BCE	14, 48, 50a, 54	23, 50b	45	39b, 58**	39a	-	10
Period IIC 2200 to 2000 BCE	8, 10, 64, 67	11, 18, 20, 26, 53, 62, 65	41	66	34	15, 25, 47, 52	18
Total	9	12	5	3	2	4	35
In Total	9 + 3= 12	12 +2= 14	5 + 4 = 9				

*unknown age; **unidentified sex

Some burials were disturbed by later burial activities, indicating that the same area was used more frequently than other parts of the cemetery. There are no evidences of cloth from the site, but the way some skeletal alignment is seen, it suggests that the person was covered with some cloth and then buried. These practices were also observed in Harappa (Kenoyer and Meadows (2016). In certain burials, it looks like the ankle or the toes are tied together.

The major problem of Farmana is bad preservation. The cemetery is situated on agriculture land. Farmers may have used a lot of fertilizer for good yield. Chemicals from these fertilizers may have increased the salinity and acidic component of the soil resulting in brittle bone conditions. Same time excavation process may have further damaged bones.

Farmana samples were tried for the isotope and DNA analysis. Unfortunately, DNA analysis was not possible as bones were in bad condition and DNA was not preserved. Strontium (Sr) and lead (Pb) isotope analysis were conducted. Biogeochemical analysis provides a complementary approach for the testing hypothesis of migration in Farmana. They were suited for identifying and determining the provenience of migrant individuals. The ratio of different isotopes has so-called "heavy" elements such as strontium (87sr/86sr) and lead (208Pb/204Pb/207Pb/204Pb/206Pb/204Pb) remain effectively the same as they pass from bedrock, into the biosphere and eventually into bone and teeth (Valentine 2016). Bones and teeth of person exhibit Sr and Pb ratios from where he or she gets exposure to water, dust, and food. Consequently, it shows the geological location of the person. If different regions can be characterized using baseline samples of fauna, plants, and soil then these can be compared against the isotopic ratios of individuals to determine their place of origin (Burton and Price 2013, Price et al 2002, Valentine 2016).

Initially, sampling was done from 21 individuals but for some individual's dental enamel was either not completely mineralized (in case of deciduous teeth) or sample was in very less quantity (Valentine, 2013) (Table 7.2). Finally, only 33 teeth from 17 individuals were considered which shows 10 development sequences of two or more data points. Selection of teeth was conducted on the basis of the tooth formation sequence. Teeth which are formed during the birth time and teeth which shows sequential development was considered. In some cases it was possible to get 2 or 3 teeth for one individual from dental chronological sequence, but some time it was not possible (Valentine *et al* 2015).

Table 7.2: Initial Farmana dental samples selected for the isotope analysis.

Individual	Age	Sex
2	Around 50 y	F
5	3.5-4 years	-
6	40-45 years	F
11	45±5 years	F
14	around 25 y	M
15	around 2 y	-
18	40-45 years	F
20	35-40 years	F
23	18 - 25 years	F
26	40-45 years	F
39b	45-50 years	M
41	7-8 years	-
45	13-15 years	-
47	7-8 years	-
52	Around 3.5 y	-
54	Around 30 y	M
58	Around 20 y	?
62	Around 15 y	F
65	30 ± 5 years	?
66	around 50 y	M
67	around 35 y	M

On the basis of dental isotope analysis, it was observed that Farmana cemetery at the site represent first migrant who were migrated at young age (3- 5 years) from distance places to the town (Valentine et al 2015, Valentine 2016). There are lot of unsolved questions regarding this early age migrations.

It was very difficult to observe sex-wise differences in cranial morphology as very few skulls provided the craniometric observations. Only two males gave cranial indices in comparison with seven females. Almost all females have a long or very long head. In nasal index six females come under the broad nose category and within two males, one is with a narrow nose and one with the very broad nose. Therefore, it is difficult to say that female belongs to one type or similar type of facial features in contrast to males. It seems like a lot of mixed traits being present, representing different people.

Interestingly in Farmana, skeletons in cemetery belong to old females and young males. There are six young males in comparison with young females (3 individuals). The opposite trend is seen on the older individuals where females are more represented; 3 in middle aged category and 5 in old age in comparison with 1 middle aged male and 2 in old age individuals. It is an interesting scenario and attempt was made to understand any relation between this pattern and pathological lesions found in the skeletal assemblage. Only in one case individual number 64, shows vertebral lipping at young age of 20 years which may reflect stress on the vertebral column.

The average male stature is 173.03 cm but the tallest individual is 187.44 cm tall (skeleton 25). For female 166.07 cm is average, but skeleton 11 is 177.63 cm.

Table 7.3: Summery of age, sex and pathological observations

Burial no.	Age	Sex	Burial type	Period	Orientation	Pathology apart from dental attrition
1	18- 20y	Male	P	-	N-S	-
2	50+ y	Female	P	-	NW-SE	-
3	-	Late adolescent	P	-	N-S	-
5	3.5-4y	Child	P	-	NW-SE	-
6	40-45y	Female	P	-	NW-SE	-
8	Adult	Male	P	IIC	NW-SE	-
10	Adult	Male	P	IIC	NE-SW	-
11	Around 45±5 y	Female (?)	P	IIC	NW-SE	-
14	20- 25 y	Male	P	IIB	NW-SE	Dental fluorosis
15	Around 2 y	Child	SE	IIC	NW-SE	-
18	40-45y	Female	P	IIC	N-S	Dental Caries
20	35- 40y	Female	P	IIC	NE-SW	-
23	18 – 20 y	Female	P	IIB	N-S	Enamel hypoplasia
25	Adult	Male	SE	IIC	N-S	-
26	40-45y	Female	P	IIC	NW-SE	-
28	Around 2.5 to 3 years	Child	P	IIA	NW-SE	-
32	18-19y	Female	P	IIA	N-S	-
34	adult	Female?	SE	IIC	N-S	-
39A	Around 45 y	Female?	SE	IIB	N-S	-

Burial no.	Age	Sex	Burial type	Period	Orientation	Pathology apart from dental attrition
39B	45-50y	Male?	SE	IIB	N-S	Trauma on skull with healing in process
41	7-8y	early adolescent	P	IIC	N-S	-
45	13-15y	Adolescent	P	IIB	NW-SE	Dental fluorosis
47	7-8y	early adolescent	SE	IIC	N-S	-
48	20±5y	Male	P	IIB	NW-SE	-
50A	25y	Male	P	IIB	N-S	-
50b	Adult around 30-35	Female	P	IIB	NW-SE	-
52	3.5y	Child	SE	IIC	NW-SE	-
53	30y	Female	P	IIC	NW-SE	-
54	30-35y	Male?	P	IIB	NW-SE	Dental Caries
58	Around 20y	Unidentified	SE (clay coffin)	IIB	N-S	-
62	15y	Female?	P	IIC	N-S	-
64	20±5y	Male	P	IIC	NW-SE	Vertebral lipping, Dental Caries
65	30y	Female?	P	IIC	NE-SW	-
66	Around 50y	Male	SE	IIC	N-S	Thick cranial bones
67	35y	Male	P	IIC	NW-SE	-

As seen in table 7.3, there are not many pathologies observed from the site. Only a few anomalies were found. Other than cranial trauma to specimen 39B, an old aged male individual, from period IIB belonging to 2400 to 2200 BCE, nothing significant findings are present. There are out of 35 individuals, only two shows some nutritional stress in the form of dental hypoplasia on a young female and the thickening of cranial bones of the old male. Even the most commonly found dental caries is only seen in two individuals, one on old female and on the middle aged male. Dental fluorosis is seen on two individuals, which might indicate the exposure to excessive fluorine in the water. There are two possibilities for not having many pathologies, one the Farmana population was quite healthy or not having proper preservation of most of the skeletal elements. Considering the time span of six hundred years (2600 BCE to 2000 BCE), the occupation and population representation in the cemetery is not an ideal.

Overall the Farmana skeletal material from its burial site give glimpses about population, or the fragment of society which it represent in cemetery. It helps us to know that, like in Harappa, people from this place also had various phenotypic characters and not confining to any particular type. Unfortunately, a DNA was not possible, may be in future new improved technology will help to get a DNA which will throw light on the population once lived in Farmana.

Appendix
Preservations Charts Skeletal Remains

PRESERVATION RECORD

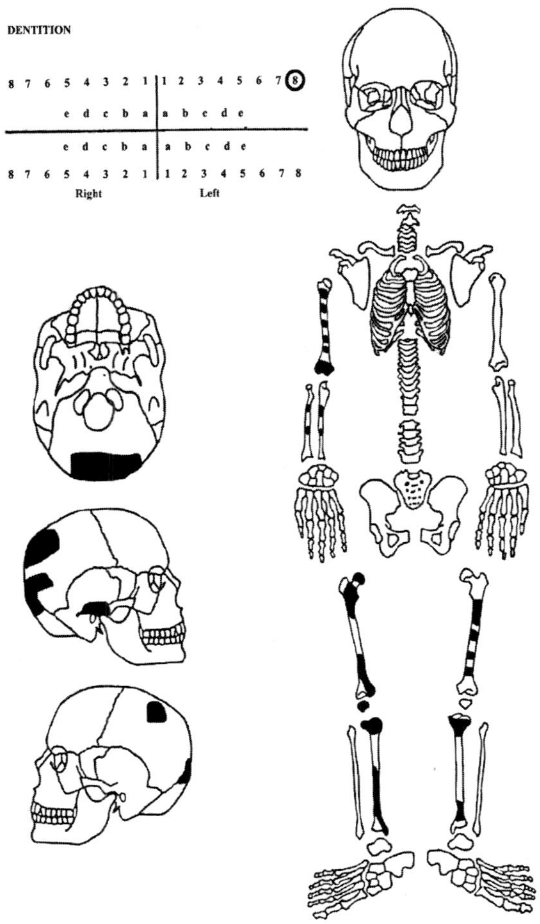

Site: Farmana Specimen no: 1

Chronological Period: Harappan

Location: ______ Burial Type: Extendeed

Excavation Date: 2007-08 Studied On: 2011-12

Age: 18-20 Years Sex: Male

PRESERVATION RECORD

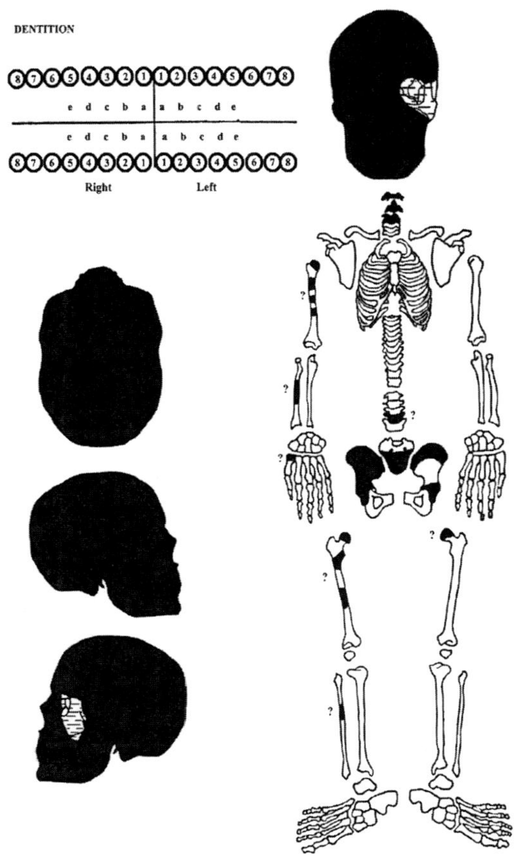

Site: Farmana Specimen no: 2

Chronological Period: Harappa

Location: ______ Burial Type: Extended

Excavation Date: 2007-08 Studied On: 2011-12

Age: 50+ Sex: Female

Observation: ______ Remarks: ______

PRESERVATION RECORD

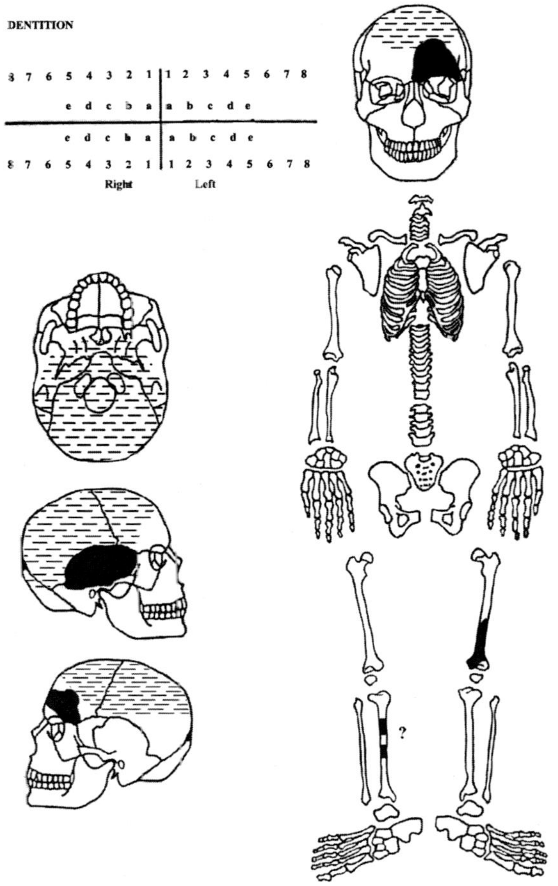

Site: Farmana Specimen no: 3

Chronological Period: Harappan

Location: Burial Type: Extended

Excavation Date: 2007-08 Studied On: 2011-12

Age: Late adolescent Sex: ?

Observation: Remarks:

PRESERVATION RECORD

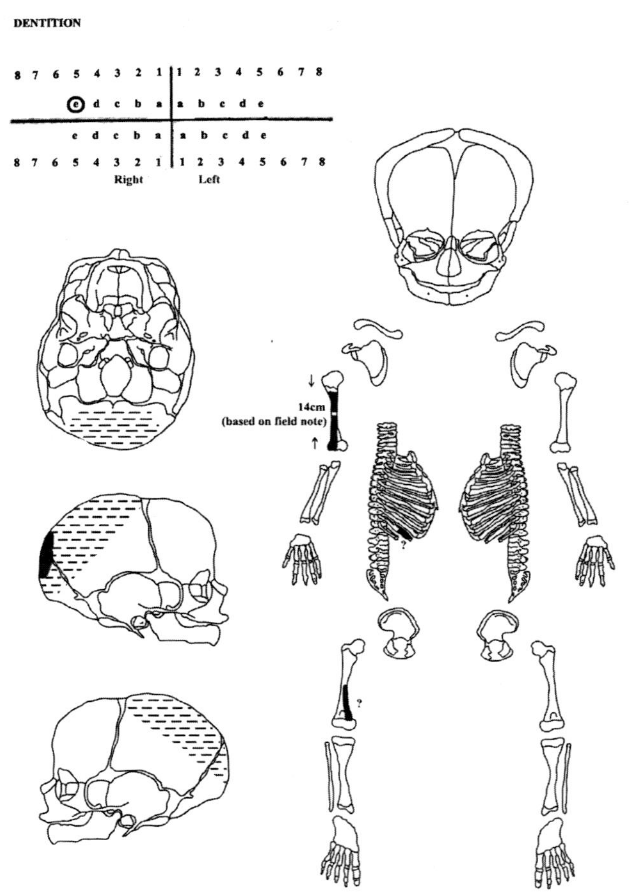

Site: Farmana Specimen no: 5

Chronological Period: Harappa

Location: Burial Type: Extended

Excavation Date: 2007-08 Studied On: 2011-12

Age: 3.5-4 Years Sex: NA

Observation: Remarks:

PRESERVATION RECORD

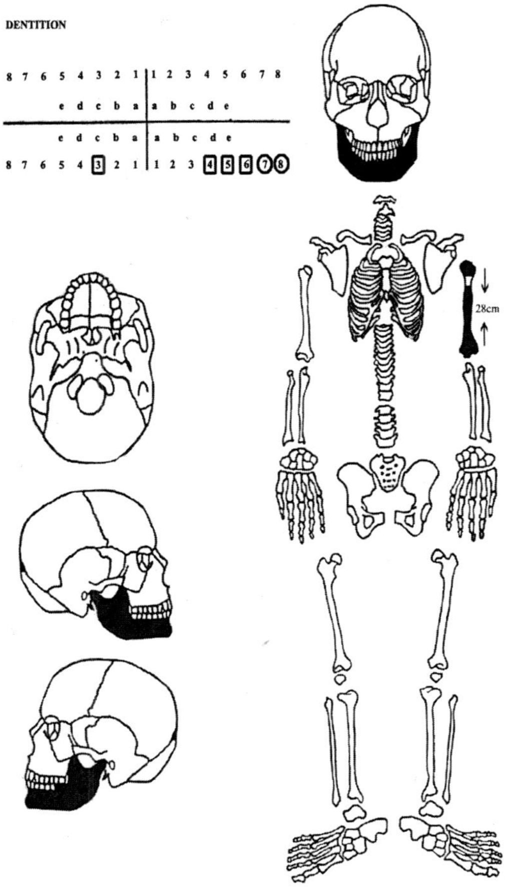

Site: Farmana **Specimen no:** 6

Chronological Period: Harappa

Location: **Burial Type:** Secondary

Excavation Date: 2007-08 **Studied On:** 2011-12

Age: 40-45 years **Sex:** Female

Observation: **Remarks:**

PRESERVATION RECORD

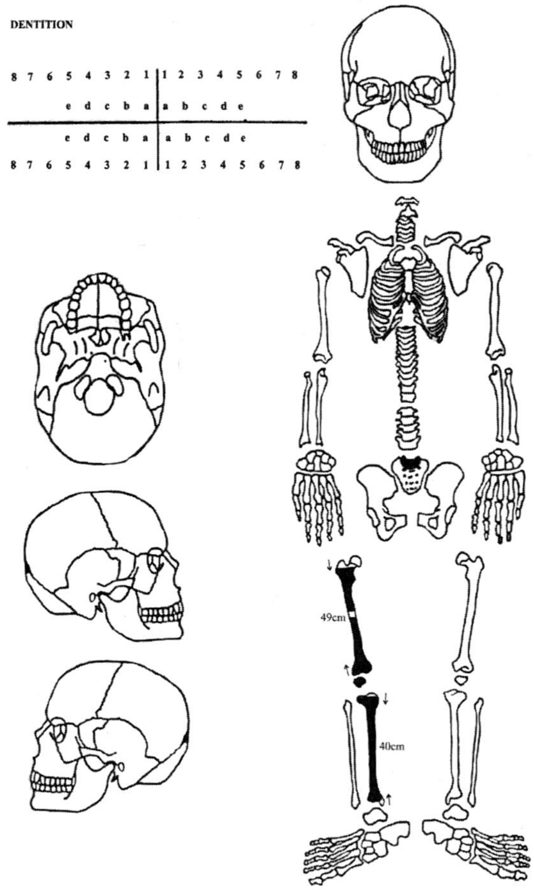

Site: Farmana **Specimen no:** 8

Chronological Period: Harappa

Location: **Burial Type:** Extended

Excavation Date: 2008-09 **Studied On:** 2011-12

Age: Adult **Sex:** Male

Observation: **Remarks:**

PRESERVATION RECORD

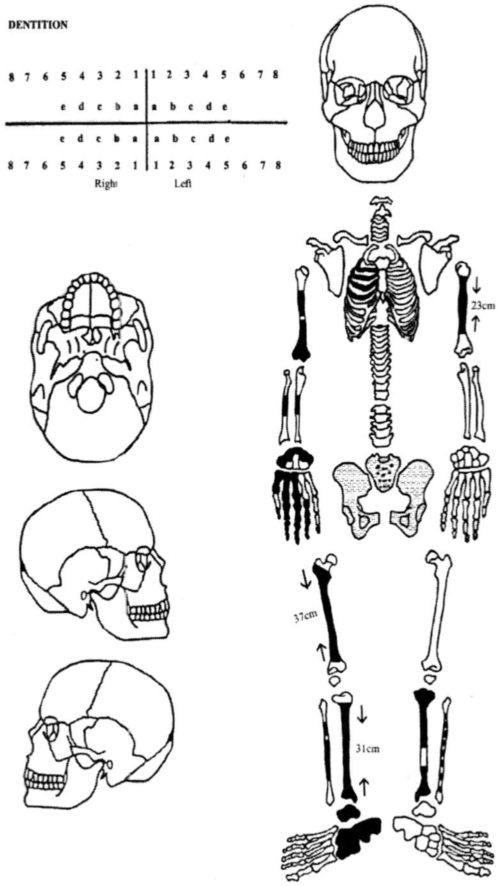

Site: Farmana **Specimen no:** 10

Chronological Period: Harappa

Location: **Burial Type:** Extended

Excavation Date: 2008-09 **Studied On:** 2011-12

Age: Adult **Sex:** Male

Observation: **Remarks:**

PRESERVATION RECORD

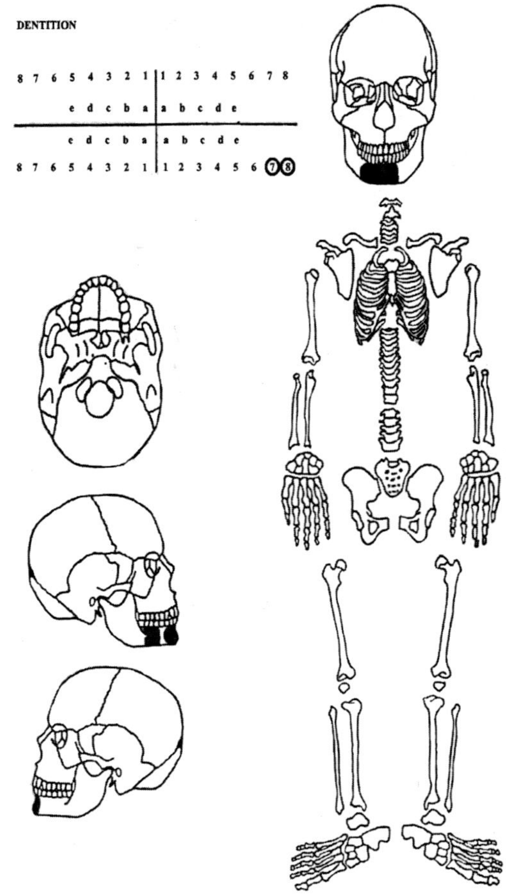

Site: Farmana **Specimen no:** 11

Chronological Period: Harappan

Location: **Burial Type:**

Excavation Date: 2008-09 **Studied On:** 2011-12

Age: 45 **Sex:** Female

Observation: **Remarks:**

PRESERVATION RECORD

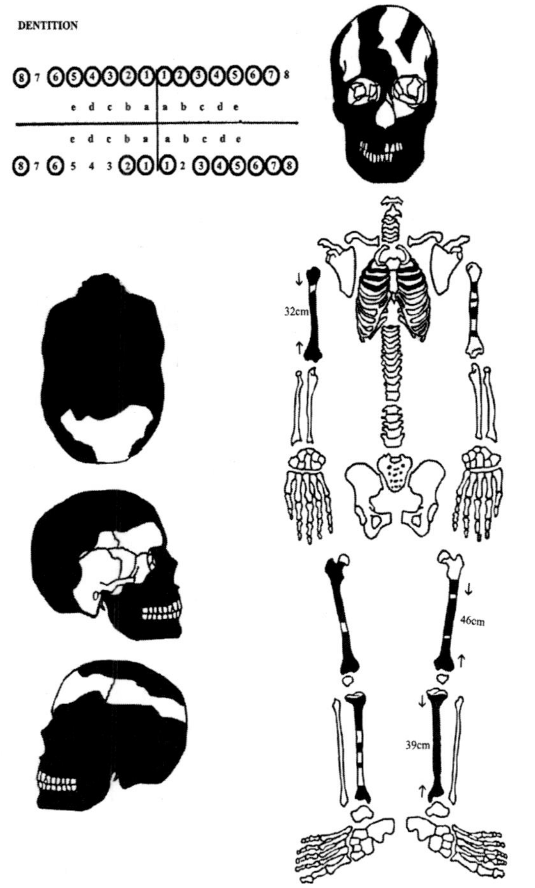

Site: Farmana **Specimen no:** 14

Chronological Period: Harappan

Location: **Burial Type:** Extemded

Excavation Date: 2008-09 **Studied On:** 2011-12

Age: 20-25 Years **Sex:** Male

Observation: **Remarks:**

PRESERVATION RECORD

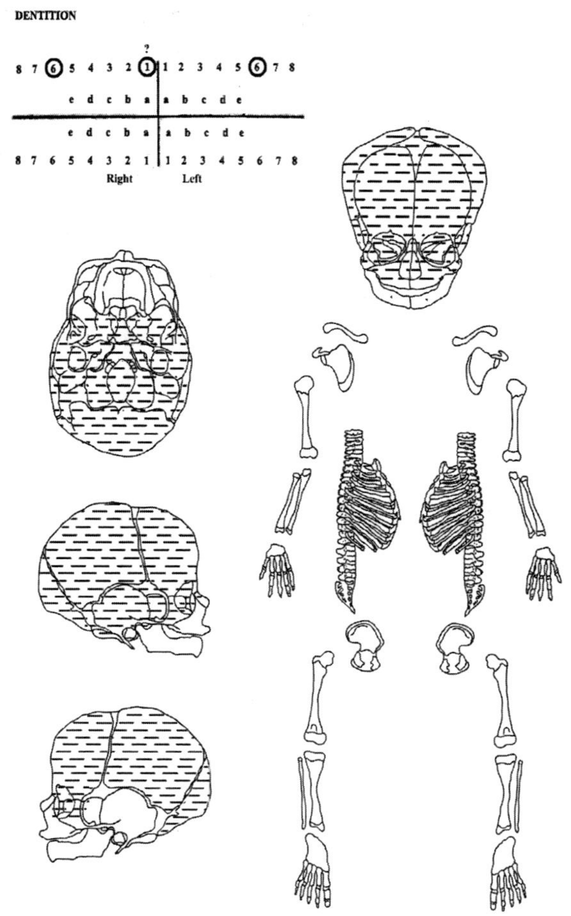

Site: Farmana **Specimen no:** 15

Chronological Period: Harappa

Location: **Burial Type:** Extended

Excavation Date: 2008-09 **Studied On:** 2011-12

Age: 2 Years **Sex:** NA

Observation: **Remarks:**

PRESERVATION RECORD

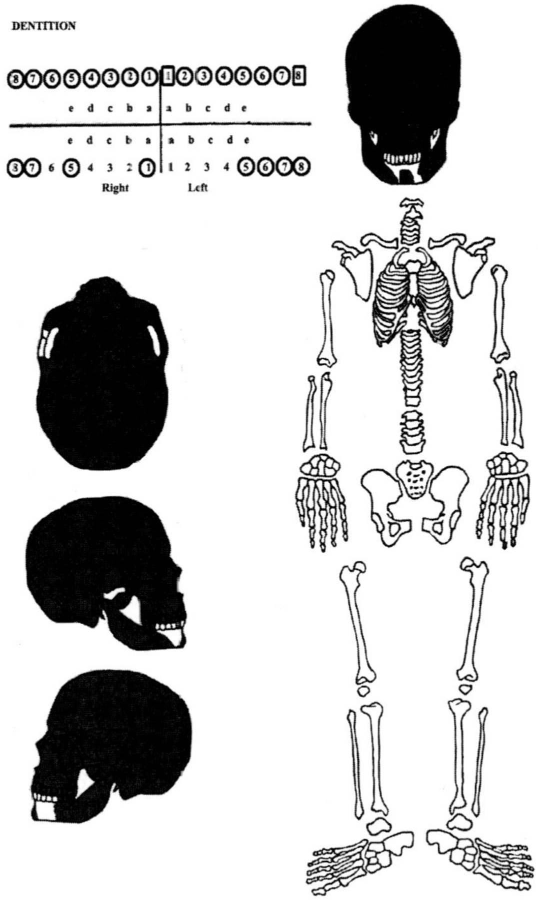

Site: Farmana **Specimen no:** 18

Chronological Period: Harappa

Location: **Burial Type:** Extended

Excavation Date: 2008-09 **Studied On:** 2011-12

Age: 40-45 Years **Sex:** Female

Observation: **Remarks:**

PRESERVATION RECORD

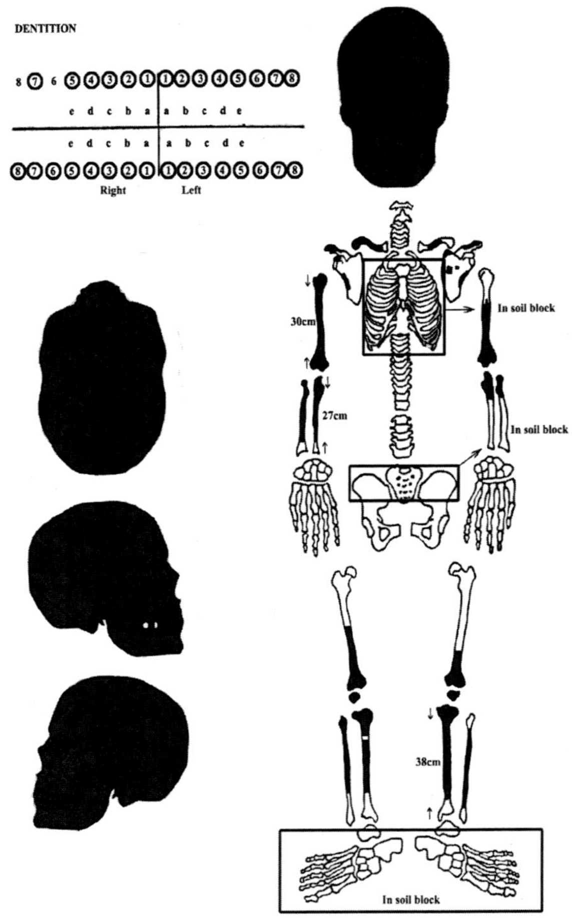

Site: Farmana **Specimen no:** 20

Chronological Period: Harappa

Location: **Burial Type:** Extended

Excavation Date: 2008-09 **Studied On:** 2011-12

Age: 35-40 years **Sex:** Female

Observation: **Remarks:**

PRESERVATION RECORD

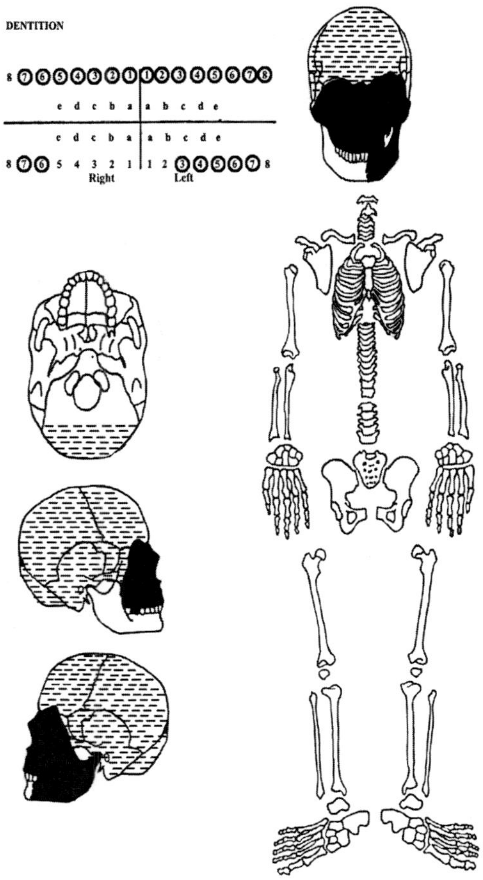

Site: Farmana Specimen no: 23

Chronological Period: Harappa

Location: Burial Type: Extended, below burial 22

Excavation Date: 2008-09 Studied On: 2011-12

Age: 18-20 Years Sex: Female

Observation: Remarks:

PRESERVATION RECORD

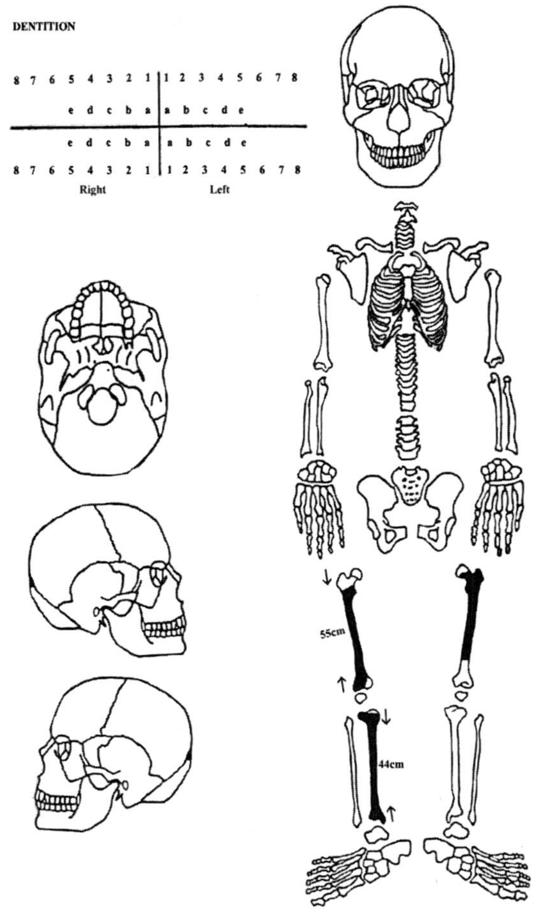

Site: Farmana Specimen no: 25

Chronological Period: Harappa

Location: Burial Type: Extended

Excavation Date: 2008-09 Studied On: 2011-12

Age: Adult Sex: Male

Observation: Remarks:

PRESERVATION RECORD

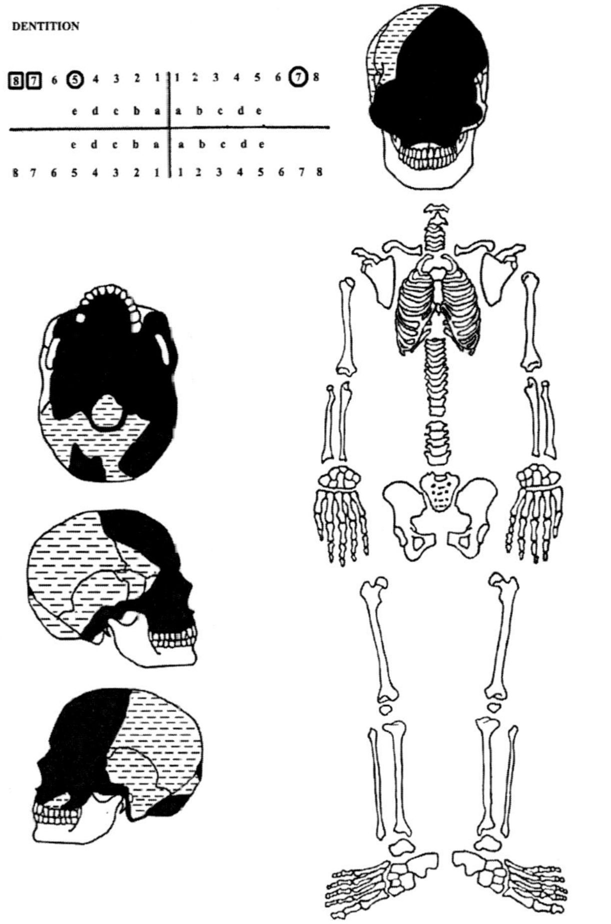

Site: Farmana Specimen no: 26

Chronological Period: Harappan

Location: Burial Type: Extended

Excavation Date: 2008-09 Studied On: 2011-12

Age: 40-45 Years Sex: Female

Observation: Remarks:

PRESERVATION RECORD

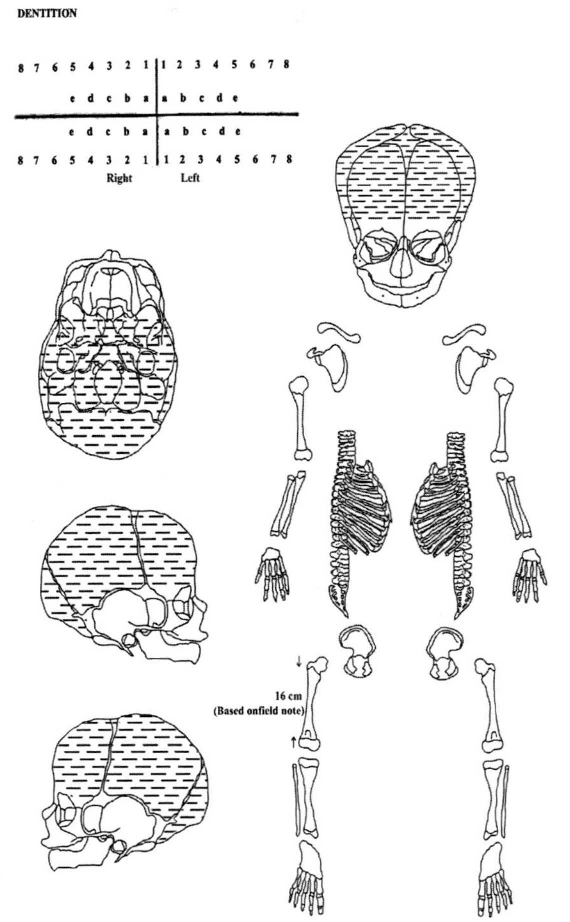

Site: Farmana Specimen no: 28

Chronological Period: Harappa

Location: Burial Type: Extended

Excavation Date: 2008-09 Studied On: 2011-12

Age: Around 2.5 to 3 years Sex: NA

Observation: Remarks:

PRESERVATION RECORD

DENTITION

8 7 6 5 4 3 2 1 | 1 2 3 4 5 6 7 8
e d c b a | a b c d e

e d c b a | a b c d e
8 7 6 5 4 3 2 1 | 1 2 3 4 5 6 7 8

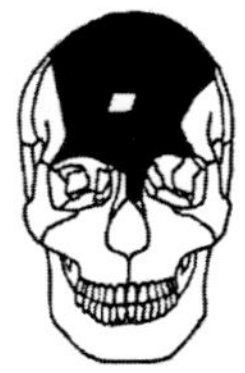

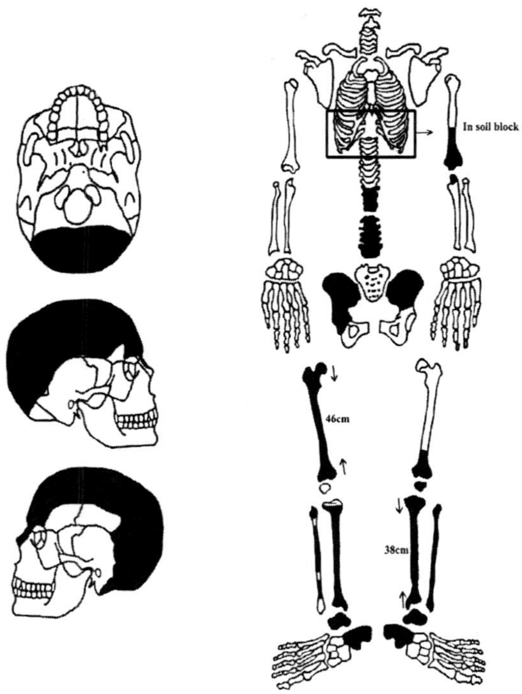

Site: Farmana **Specimen no:** 32

Chronological Period: Harappa

Location: **Burial Type:** Extended

Excavation Date: 2008-09 **Studied On:** 2011-12

Age: 18-19 years **Sex:** Female

Observation: **Remarks:**

PRESERVATION RECORD

DENTITION

8 7 6 5 4 3 2 1 | 1 2 3 4 5 6 7 8
e d c b a | a b c d e

e d c b a | a b c d e
8 7 6 5 4 3 2 1 | 1 2 3 4 5 6 7 8

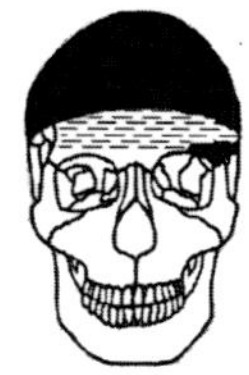

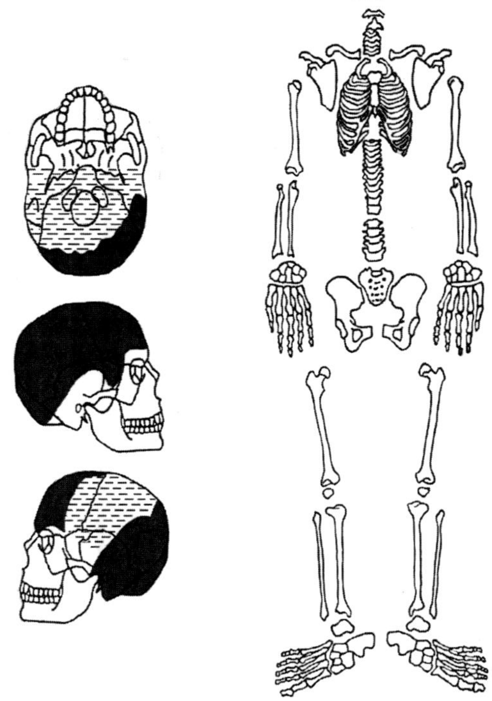

Site: Farmana **Specimen no:** 34

Chronological Period: Harappa

Location: **Burial Type:** extended

Excavation Date: 2008-09 **Studied On:** 2011-12

Age: Adult **Sex:** Female

Observation: **Remarks:**

PRESERVATION RECORD

DENTITION

8	7	6	5	4	3	2	1	1	2	3	4	5	6	7	8
			e	d	c	b	a	a	b	c	d	e			
			e	d	c	b	a	a	b	c	d	e			
8	7	6	5	4	3	2	1	1	2	3	4	5	6	7	8

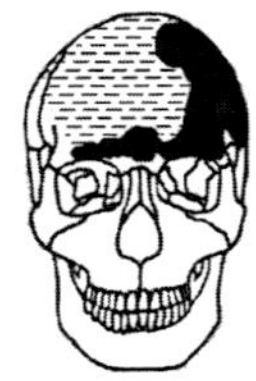

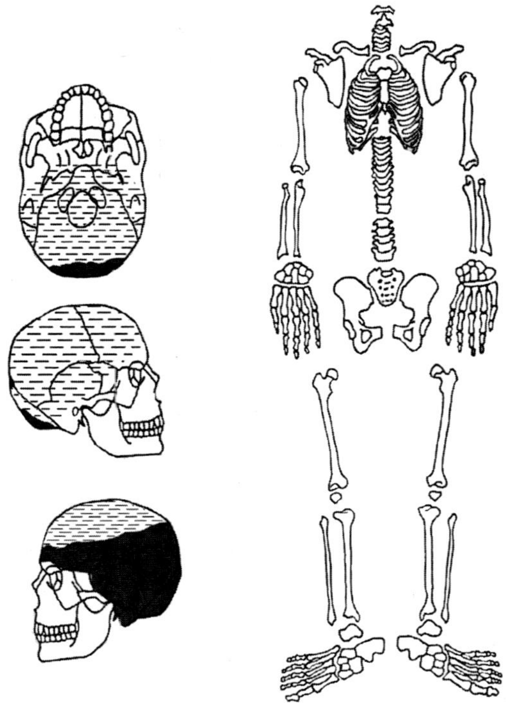

Site: Farmana Specimen no: 39A

Chronological Period: Harappa

Location: Burial Type: Secondary

Excavation Date: 2008-09 Studied On: 2011-12

Age: Around 45 years Sex: Female

Observation: Remarks:

PRESERVATION RECORD

DENTITION

8 ?	7	6	5	4	3	2	1	1	2	3	4	5	6	7	8
			e	d	c	b	a	a	b	c	d	e			
			e	d	c	b	a	a	b	c	d	e			
8 ?	7	6	5	4	3	2	1	1	2	3	4	5	6	7	8

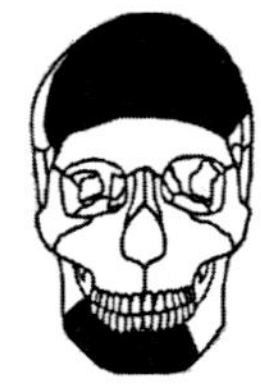

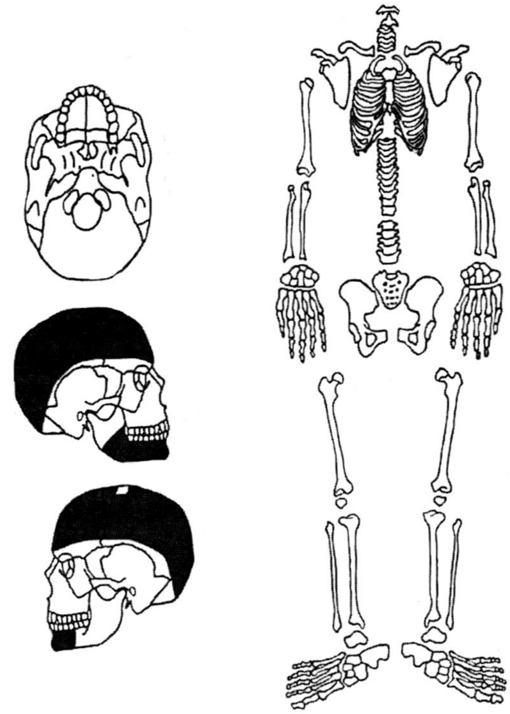

Site: Farmana Specimen no: 39B

Chronological Period: Harappa

Location: Burial Type: Secondary

Excavation Date: 2008-09 Studied On: 2011-12

Age: 45-50 Years Sex: Male

Observation: Remarks:

PRESERVATION RECORD

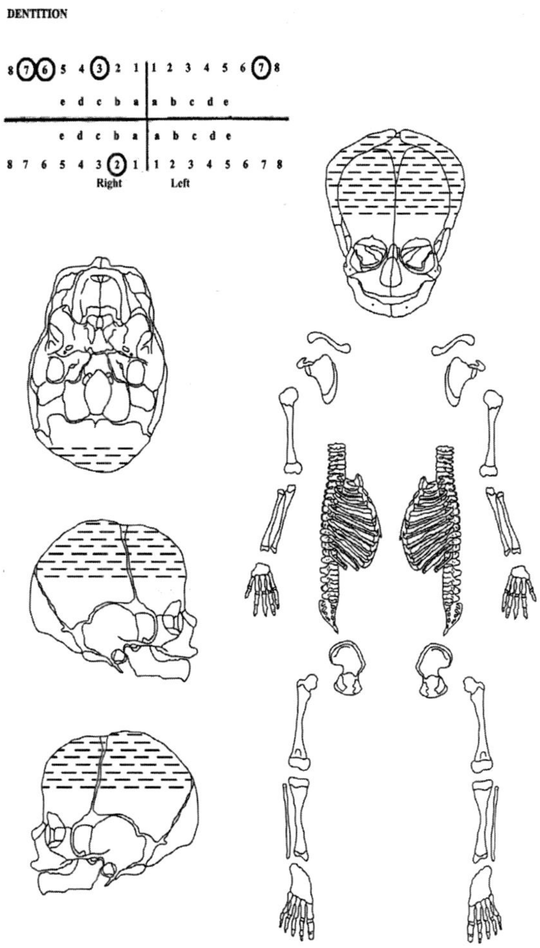

Site: Farmana | Specimen no: 41

Chronological Period: Harappa

Location: | Burial Type: Extended

Excavation Date: 2008-09 | Studied On: 2011-12

Age: 7-8 Years | Sex: NA

Observation: | Remarks:

PRESERVATION RECORD

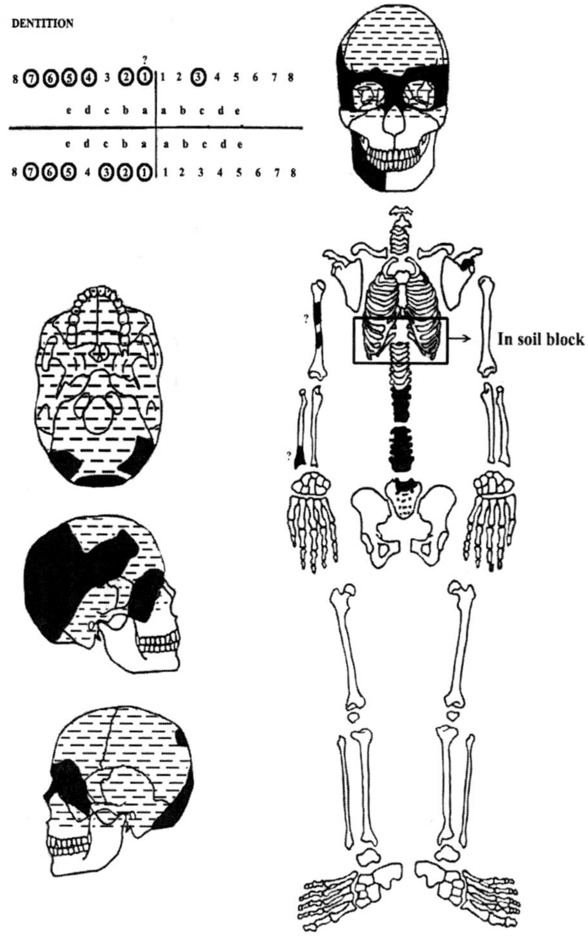

Site: Farmana | Specimen no: 45

Chronological Period: Harappa

Location: | Burial Type: Extendeed

Excavation Date: 2008-09 | Studied On: 2011-12

Age: 13-15 Years | Sex:

Observation: | Remarks:

PRESERVATION RECORD

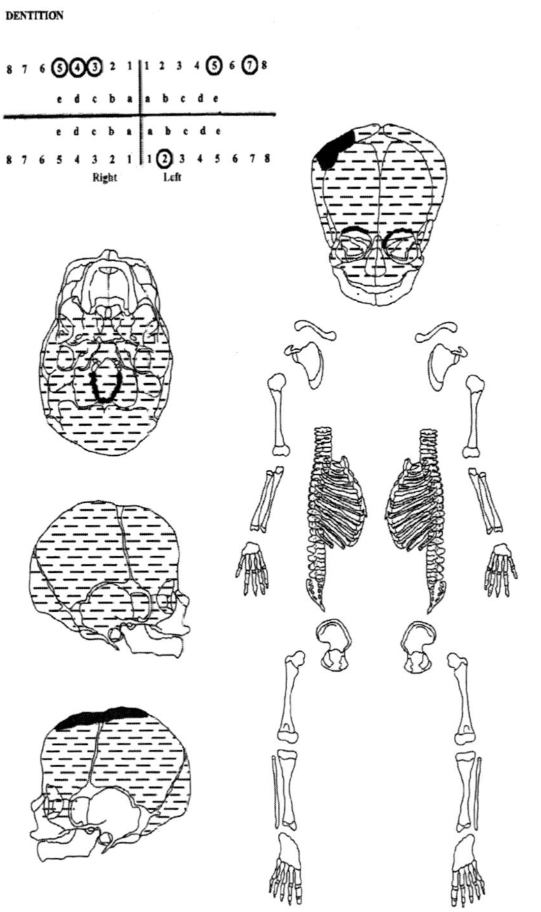

Site: Farmana Specimen no: 47

Chronological Period: Harappa

Location: Burial Type: Extended

Excavation Date: 2008-09 Studied On: 2011-12

Age: 7-8 Years Sex: NA

Observation: Remarks:

PRESERVATION RECORD

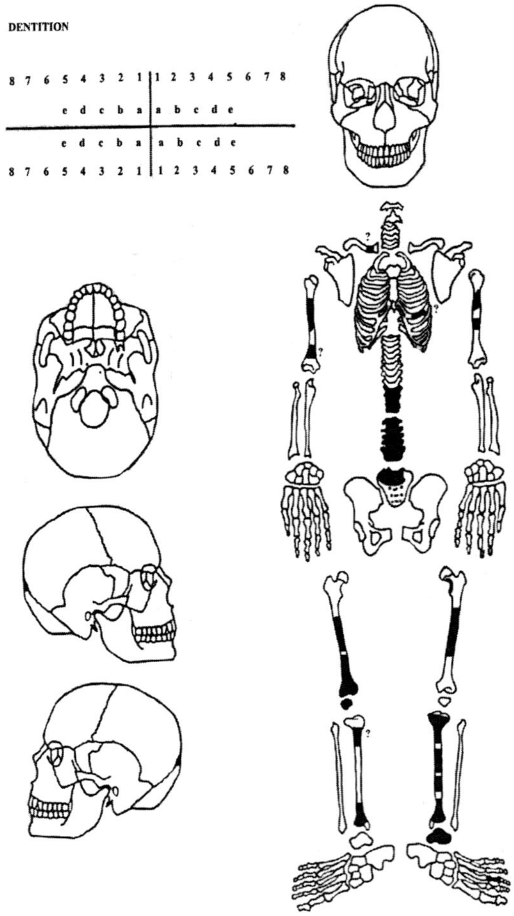

Site: Farmana Specimen no: 48

Chronological Period: Harappa

Location: Burial Type: Extended

Excavation Date: 2008-09 Studied On: 2011-12

Age: 20-25 Years Sex: Male

Observation: Remarks:

PRESERVATION RECORD

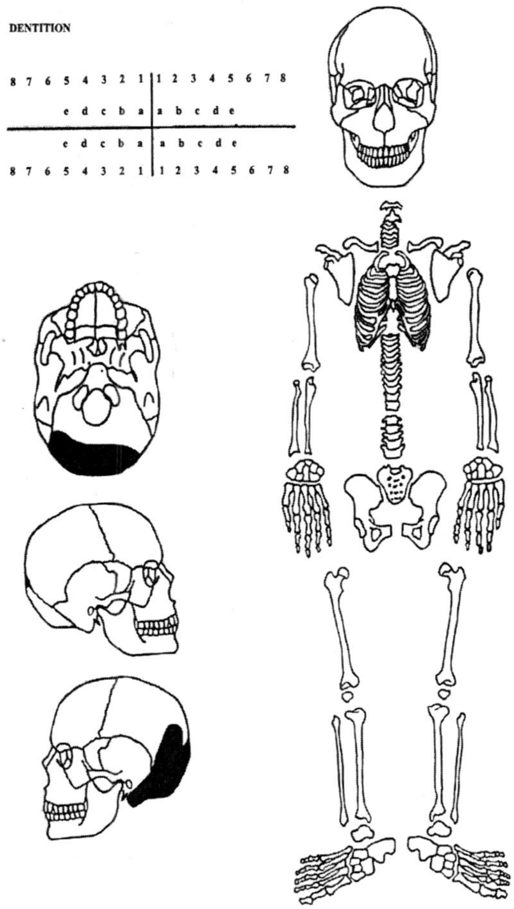

Site: Farmana Specimen no: 50A

Chronological Period: Harappa

Location: ______ Burial Type: ______

Excavation Date: 2008-09 Studied On: 2011-12

Age: 25 Years Sex: Male

Observation: ______ Remarks: ______

PRESERVATION RECORD

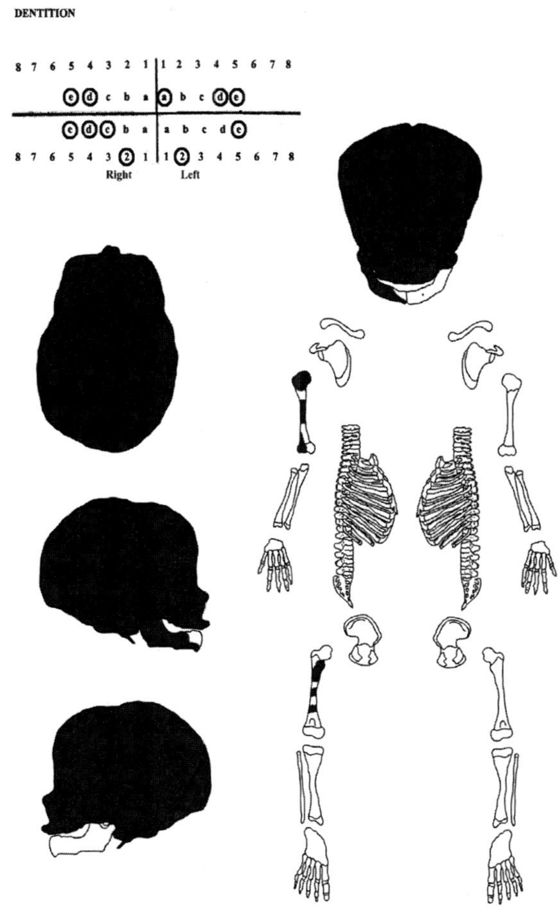

Site: Framana Specimen no: 52

Chronological Period: Harappa

Location: ______ Burial Type: Secondary

Excavation Date: 2008-09 Studied On: 2011-12

Age: 3.5 Years Sex: NA

Observation: ______ Remarks: ______

PRESERVATION RECORD

DENTITION

8 7 6 5 4 3 2 1 | 1 2 3 4 5 6 7 8
e d c b a | a b c d e

e d c b a | a b c d e
8 7 6 5 4 3 2 1 | 1 2 3 4 5 6 7 8

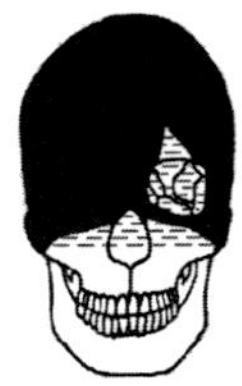

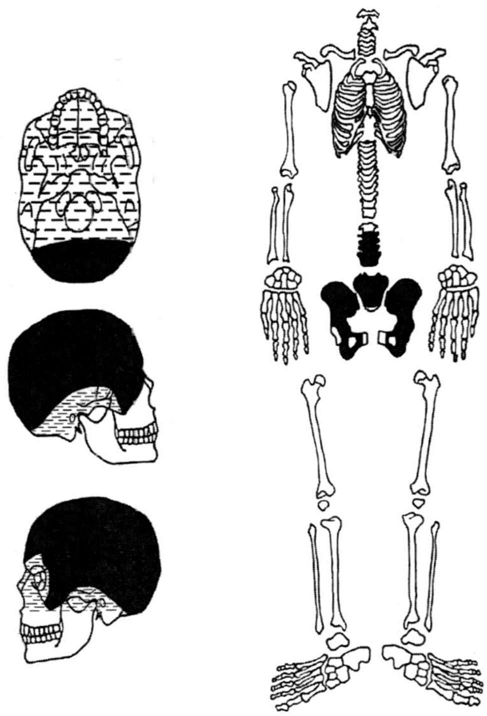

Site: Farmana Specimen no: 53

Chronological Period: Harappa

Location: Burial Type: Extended

Excavation Date: 2008-09 Studied On: 2011-12

Age: 30 Years Sex: Female

Observation: Remarks:

PRESERVATION RECORD

DENTITION

8 7 6 5 4 3 2 1 | 1 2 3 4 5 6 7 8
e d c b a | a b c d e

e d c b a | a b c d e
8 7 (6) 5 4 3 2 1 | 1 2 3 4 5 6 7 8

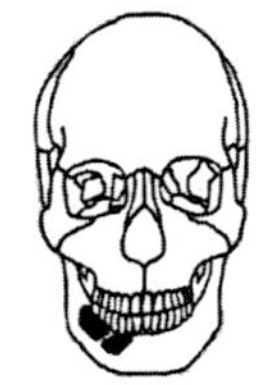

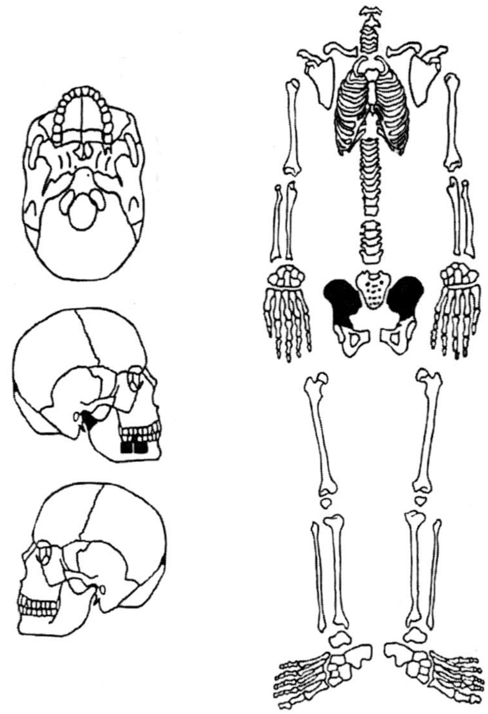

Site: Farmana Specimen no: 54

Chronological Period: Harappa

Location: Burial Type: Extended, facing to left

Excavation Date: 2008-09 Studied On: 2011-12

Age: 30-35Years Sex: Male

Observation: Remarks:

PRESERVATION RECORD

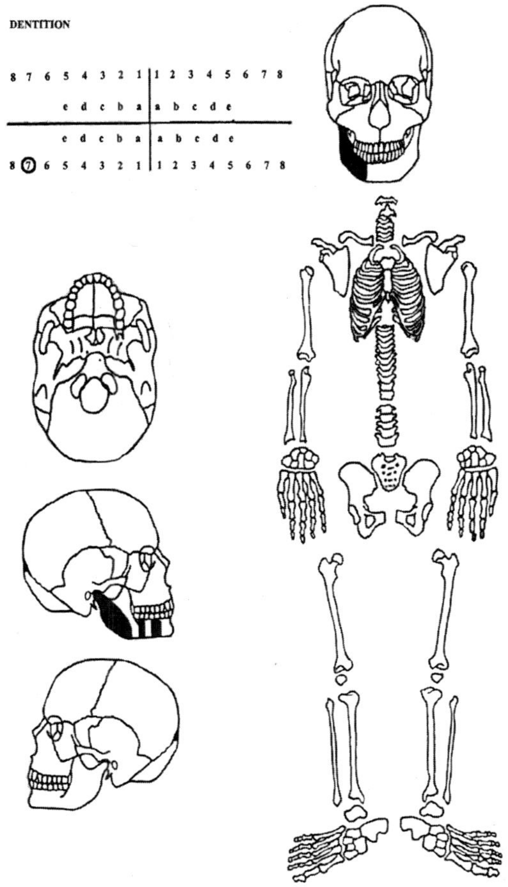

Site: Farmana **Specimen no:** 58

Chronological Period: Harappa

Location: **Burial Type:** Secondary

Excavation Date: 2008-09 **Studied On:** 2011-12

Age: 20 Years **Sex:** ?

Observation: **Remarks:**

PRESERVATION RECORD

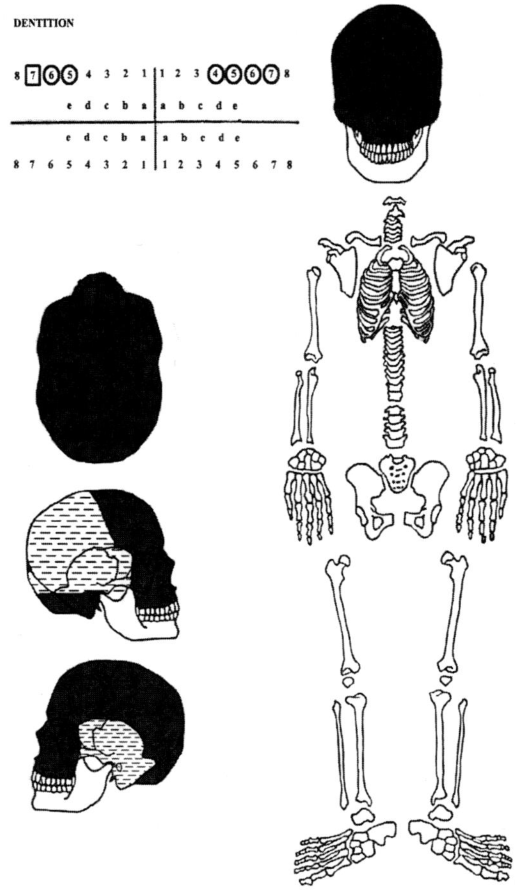

Site: Farmana **Specimen no:** 62

Chronological Period: Harappa

Location: **Burial Type:** Extended

Excavation Date: 2008-09 **Studied On:** 2011-12

Age: 15 Years **Sex:** Female

Observation: **Remarks:**

PRESERVATION RECORD

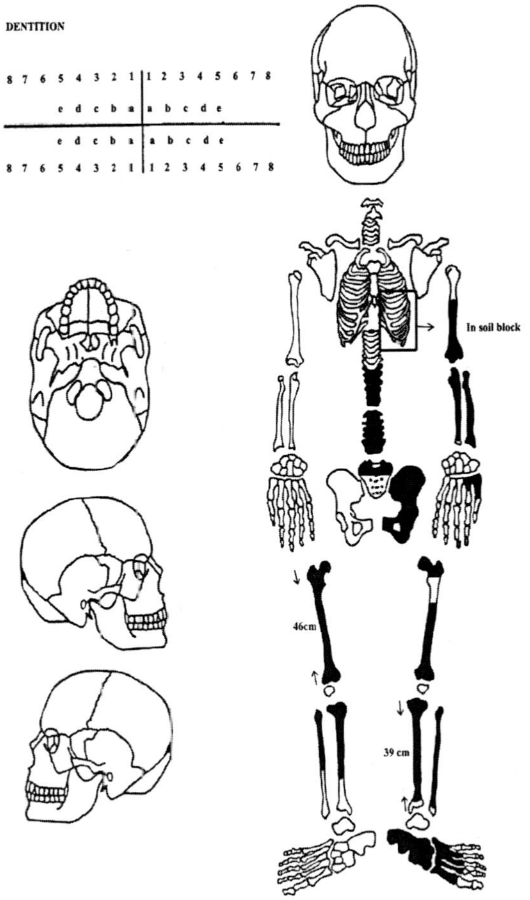

Site: Farmana Specimen no: 64

Chronological Period: Harappa

Location: Burial Type: Exteded

Excavation Date: 2008-09 Studied On: 2011-12

Age: 20 Years Sex: Male

Observation: Remarks:

PRESERVATION RECORD

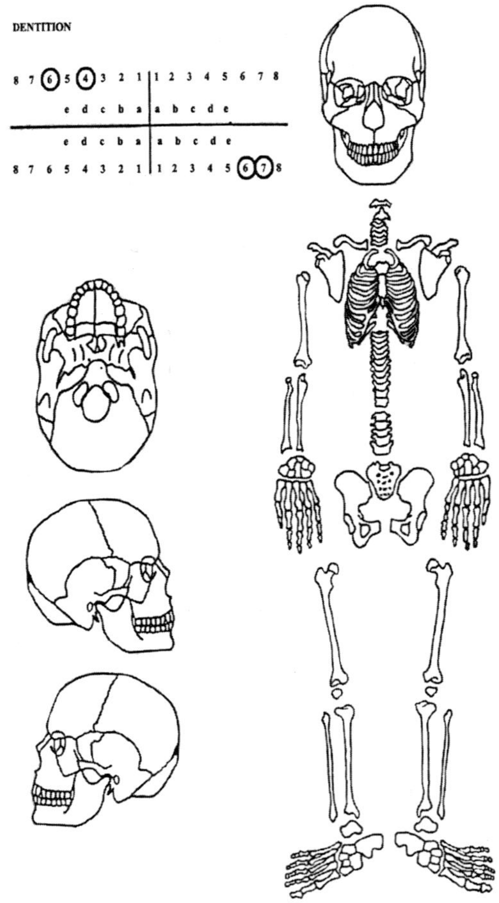

Site: Farmana Specimen no: 65

Chronological Period: Harappa

Location: Burial Type: Extended

Excavation Date: 2008-09 Studied On: 2011-12

Age: 30 Years Sex: Female (field note)

Observation: Remarks:

PRESERVATION RECORD

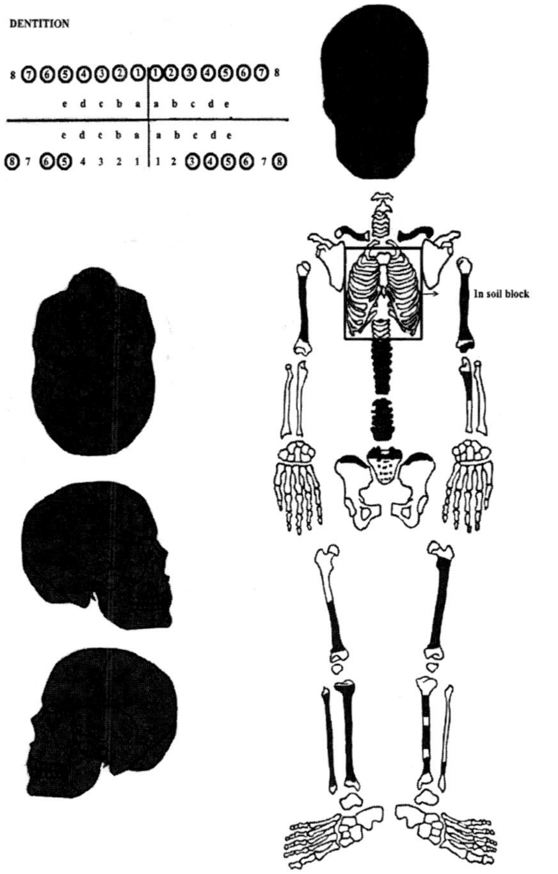

Site: Farmana Specimen no: 67

Chronological Period: Harappa

Location: Burial Type: Extended

Excavation Date: 2008-09 Studied On: 2011-12

Age: 35 Years Sex: Male

Observation: Remarks:

PRESERVATION RECORD

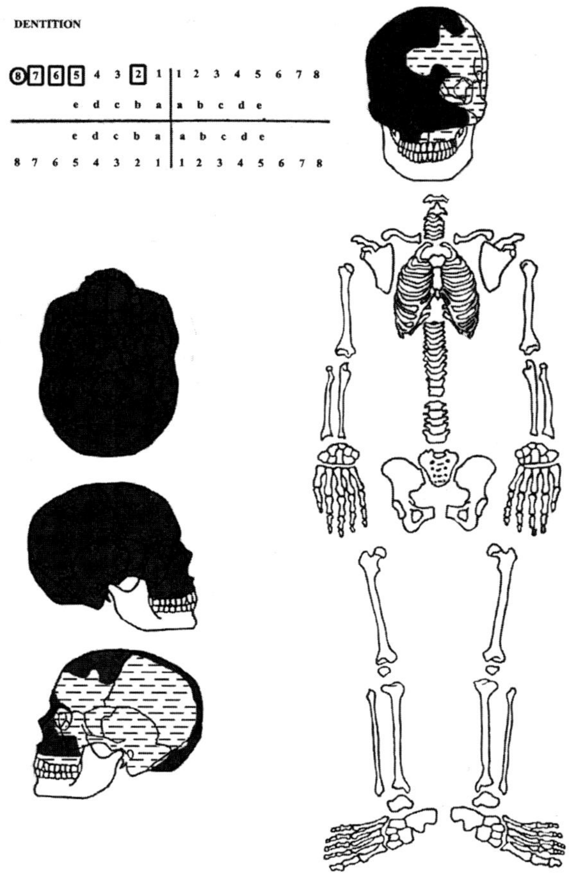

Site: Farmana Specimen no: 66

Chronological Period: Harappa

Location: Burial Type: Secondary

Excavation Date: 2008-09 Studied On: 2011-12

Age: 50 Years Sex: Male

Observation: Remarks:

Bibliography

Bennike, P. 2008. Trauma. *Advances in Human Palaeopathology* (Eds. R. Pinhasi and S. Mays), Pp 309 – 328. Willy and Sons: England.

Bisht, R.S. 1993. (2nd edition). Excavations at Banawali: 1974-77, in *Harappan Civilization*, (Ed. Gregory Possehl), New Delhi.

Brothwell, D.R. 1981. *Digging of Bones.* London: The British Museum.

Buikstra, J.E. and D.H. Ubelaker. 1994. *Standards for Data Collection from Human Skeletal Remains.* Arkansas: Arkansas Archaeological Survey Research Series, No.44.

Burton J.H. and Price T.D. 2013. Seeking the local 87Sr/86Sr ratio to determine geographic origins of humans. In (Eds. R.A. Armitage and J.H. Burton). pp. 309–320. *Archaeological chemistry VIII.* Washington DC: American Chemical Society.

Cooper C. 1998. Epidemiology. In (Eds.J Klippel and P Dieppe) *Rheumatology*, pp. 2.1-2.8, 2nd edition. London: Mosby.

Dahlberg, A.A. 1963. Analysis of the American Indian Dentition, in *Dental Anthropology* (Eds. D.R. Brothwell), Vol. 5, pp. 149-177. Pergamon Press: London.

Danino, M. 2016. Aryan and the Indus Civilization: Archaeological, Skeletal and Molecular Evidence. In *A companion to South Asia in the Past* (Eds. G. Robbin Schug and S.R. Walimbe). Pp.205 – 224. Willy Blackwell: Oxford.

Dean, H. (1942) The investigation of physiological effects by the epidemiological method. In (Ed. F.R. Moulton), *Fluorine and Dental Health, American Association for the Advancement of Science No. 19*, Washington, D.C, pp 23-31

Dieppe P, and Lim K. 1998. Clinical features and diagnostic problems. In *Rheumatology* (Eds. J Klippel and P Dieppe) pp. 3.1-3.16, 2nd Edition. London: Mosb,

Fejerskov O., Manji F., and Baelum V. 1990. The nature and mechanisms of dental fluorosis in man. *Journal of Dental Research*, 69: 692-700.

Flemming Mr P, and Gudjansson S. (1932). Massive fluorosis of bones and ligaments. *Acta Radiologica* 13:269-294

Guha B.S. and P.C. Basu. 1938. Report on the Human Remains Excavated at Mohenjodaro in 1928-29, in *Further Excavations at Mohenjodaro* (Ed. J.H. Mackay), pp.613-638. New Delhi: Government of India.

Hemphill B.E., J.R. Lukacs, and K.A.R.Kennedy. 1991. Biological Adaptations and Affinities of Bronze Age Harappans, in *Harappan excavation 1986-1990: A Multidisciplinary Approach to Third Millennium Urbanism* (R.H. Meadow Ed.), pp.137-182. Madison: Prehistory Press.

Hillson, S. 2001. Recording Dental Caries in Archaeological Human Remains. *International Journal of Osteoarchaeology* 11: 249–289

Keith, A. 1931. *The Ancient Mesopotamia of India. Town planning 5000 years ago at Mohenjo-daro.* Illustrated London News, 19 December, pp. 1000-1004.

Kennedy K.A.R. 1982. Paleodemographic Perspectives of Social Structural Change in Harappans Society, in *Anthropology in Pakistan: Recent Socio-cultural and Archaeological Perspectives* (S.Pastner and L.Flam Eds.), pp. 211-218. Cornell: Cornell University, South Asia Occasional Papers and Theses.

Kennedy K.A.R. 1984a. Biological Adaptations and Affinities of Mesolithic South Asians, in *The People of South Asia: The Biological Anthropology of India, Pakistan and Nepal* (J.R.Lukacs Ed.), pp. 29-57. New York: Plenum Press.

Kennedy K.A.R. 1984b. Trauma and Disease in the Ancient Harappans Recent Assessments of the Skeletal Record, in *Frontiers of the Indus Civilization* (B.B. Lal and S.P. Gupta Eds.), pp. 425-436. New Delhi: Books and Books.

Kennedy K.A.R. 1995. Identification of Sacrificial and Massacre Victims in Archaeological Sites: the Skeletal Evidence, *Man and Environment* XIX(1-2):247-251.

Kennedy, K.A R. 2003. God-Apes and Fossil Men: Palaeoanthropology of South Asia. University of Michigan Press: USA

Kenoyer, J.M. and R.H. Meadow. 2016. Excavations at Harappa, 1986-2010: New Insights on the Indus Civilization and Harappan Burial Traditions. In A companion to South Asia in the Past (Eds. G. Robbin Schug and S.R. Walimbe). Wiley Blackwell:

Khan, F.A. 1968. Exploration in Pakistan, Part, Details of archaeological excavation. Pakistan Quaternary 15 (2): 1-7.

Larsen, C.S. 1997. *Bioarchaeology: Interpreting Behaviour from Human Skeleton.* United Kingdom: Cambridge University press.

Louise Scheuer and Sue Black OBE. 2004. *The Juvenile Skeleton.* Elsevier Academic Press: London

Lovell, N. C. 1997. Trauma Analysis in Paleopathology, in Yearbook of Physical Anthropology 40:139–170

Lukacs J.R. 1989. Dental Paleopathology: Methods for Reconstructing Dietary Patterns. In Reconstruction of Life from the Skeleton (Iscan M.Y. and K. A. R. Kennedy Eds.). Alan R. Liss, Inc., New York: 261-286.

MacKay E.J.H. (Ed.). 1938. *Further Excavations at Mohenjo-daro.* New Delhi: Government of India.

Mandel, I.D. 1979. Dental Caries: Although we seem to be paying for the sweet life through the teeth, resistance to caries is possible, both as a natural and an induced phenomenon. American Scientist, Vol. 67, No. 6, pp. 680-688

Marshall J. 1931. *Mohenjodaro and the Indus Civilization.* London: Probisthain

Martin, R. and K. Saller 1957. *Lehrbuch Der Anthropologie.* Band 1. Stuttgart: Gustav Fsher Verlog.

Mays, S. 2008. Metabolic Bone Disease in Advances in Human Palaeopathology (Eds. R. Pinhasi and S.Mays). John Wiley & Sons: England.

Moorrees, C.F.A. 1957a. *The Aleut Dentition.* Cambridge, Massachusetts: Harvard University Press.

Moorrees, C.F.A. 1957b. Mesiodistal Crown Diameters of the Deciduous and Permanent Teeth in Individuals, *Journal of Dental Research* 36: 39-47.

Mushrif-Tripathy, V. and S.R. Walimbe. 2006. *Human skeletal remains from Chalcolithic Nevasa: Osteobiographic Analysis.* Bar International Review: London.

Mushrif-Tripathy, V., K.S. Chakraborty and S. Lahiri. 2016. Where Are They Now? The Human Skeletal Remains from India in *A Companion to South Asia in the Past.* (Eds G. R. Schug and S. R. Walimbe), Pp. 496- 533. John Wiley & Sons, Inc, Hoboken, NJ.

Olivier, G. 1969. *Practical Anthropology.* Springfield, Illinois: Charles C.Thomas.

Ortner, D.J. and W.G.J. Putschar 2003. *Identification of Pathological Condition in Human Skeletal Remains.* Washington, D.C.: Smithsonian Institution.

Pindborg, J.J. 1970. *Pathology of the Dental Hard Tissues.* Philadelphia: W. B. Saunders Company.

Potter, R.H.Y., R.S. Corruccini, and L.J. Greene. 1981. Variance of Occlusion Traits in Twins, *Journal of Craniofacial Developmental Biology* 1: 217-227.

Price TD, Burton JH, Bentley RA (2002) The characterization of biologically available strontium isotope ratios for the study of prehistoric migration. Archaeometry 44(1): 117–135.

Resnick D. (1995) Disorders due to medications and other chemical agents. In: Resnick D. (ed.), Diagnosis of Bone and Joint Disorders, 3rd. Saunders, Philadelphia, pp. 3309-3342.

Roberts AC. 2009. Human Remains in Archaeology: a handbook. Oxford: Information Press.

Roberts, C. and K. Manchester 1995. The Archaeology of Disease. Ithaca, NY: Cornell University Press.

Sankaran B, and Gadekar N. (1964). Skeletal fluorosis. In Proceedings of the First European Bone and Tooth Symposium, Oxford, 1963.Oxford: Pergamon Press.

Vasant Shinde, T. Osada, A. Uesugi Manmohan Kumar. 2010. *Harappan Necropolis at Farmana in the Ghaggar Basin*, Special Report No. 4 of the Indian Archaeological Society: New Delhi.

Shinde, V., T. Osada, Manmohan Kumar. 2011. Excavations at Farmana 2006-08. Human Past. Indus Project, Research Institute for Humanity and Nature, Kyoto, Japan.

Shinde, V., T. Osada, M. M. Sharma, A. Uesugi and Manmohan Kumar 2008a. A Report on Excavations at Farmana 2007-08. In T. Osada and A. Uesugi (eds.) Occasional Paper 6: Linguistics, Archeology and the Human Past. Indus Project, Research Institute for Humanity and Nature, Kyoto, Japan

Shinde, V., T. Osada, M.M. Sharma, A. Uesugi, T. Uno, H. Maemoku, P. Shirvalkar, S.S. Deshpande, A. Kulkarni, A. Sarkar, A. Reddy, V. Rao and V. Dangi. 2008b. "Exploration in the Ghaggar Basin and Excavation at Girawad, Farmana (Rohtak district) and Mitathal (Bhiwani district), Haryana, India", in T. Osada and A. Uesugi (eds.) Occasional Paper: Linguistics, Archaeology and the Human Past 3. Indus Project, Research Institute for Humanity and Nature, Kyoto pp.77-158.

Sigh I. P. and M.K. Basin 1968. *Anthropometry*. Bharti Bhawan: New Delhi

Solomon L. 2001. Clinical features of osteoarthritis. In S Ruddy, E Harris Jr., and C Sledge (eds,): Kelley's Textbook of Rheumatology, 6th. Philadelphia: Saunders, pp. 1409-1418.

Steckel Richard H. and J. C. Rose (Eds.). 2002. The Backbone of History: Health and Nutrition in the Western Hemisphere. University of Cambridge: UK

Stewart, T.D. 1979. *Essentials of Forensic Anthropology.* Springfield, Illinois: C. Thomas.

Trotter, M. 1970. Estimation of Stature From Intact Long Limb Bones, in *Personal Identification in Mass Disasters* (T.D. Stewart Ed.), pp.71-83. Washington D.C.: National Museum of Natural History.

Turner CGII, Cadien JD. 1969. Dental chipping in Aeuts, Eskimos and Indians. American Journal of Physical Anthropology 31: 303–310.

Turner, C.J. II, C.R. Nichol and C.R. Scott 1991. Scoring Procedure for Key Morphological Traits of the Permanent Dentition: The Arizona State University Dental Anthropology System, in *Advances in Dental Anthropology* (M.A. Kelley and C.S. Larsen, Eds.), pp. 13-31, New York: Wiley Liss. Inc.

Valentine B. 2016. More than Origins: Refining Migration in the Indus Civilization. In A companion to South Asia in the Past (Eds. G. Robbin Schug and S.R. Walimbe). Willy Blackwell: Oxford. Pp.187 – 204.

Valentine, B. Kamenov, G. D., Kenoyer, J.M., Shinde, V., Mushrif-Tripathy, V., Otarola-Castillo, E., Krigbaum, J. 2015 Evidence for Patterns of Selective Urban Migration in the Greater Indus Valley (2600- 1900 BC): A Lead and Strontium Isotope Mortuary Analysis. PLoS ONE 10(4): e0123103. doi:10.1371/journal.pone.0123103

Waldorn, T.2008. *Paleopathology*. New York: Cambridge University Press.

Walimbe S.R. 1993. The Aryans: The Physical Anthropological Approach. In Deo S.B.,Kamath S. Editors. *The Aryan Problem*. Pune: Bhartiya Itihasa Sankalana Samiti. Pp. 108- 115.

Walimbe, S. R. 1986. Paleodemography of Protohistoric Daimabad, in *Daimabad: 1976-79*, (S.A.Sali, Ed.), pp. 641-740. New Delhi: Archaeological Survey of India.

Walimbe S. R. 2014. Human skeletoal biology. In Chakaravarthi DK, Lal M, Editors. History of ancient India. Volume 2: Protohistoric Foundations. New Delhi: Aryan Book International.

Wheeler, R.E.M. 1968. The Indus Civilization. Supplementary volume to the Cambridge History of India. 3rd edition. Cambridge: Cambridge University Press.

Wolpoff, M.H. 1971. *Metric Trends in Hominid Dental Evolution.* Case Western Reserve University, Studies in Anthropology.

Index